ASTRO CITY
...SSION

KURT BUSIEK
Writer

BRENT ERIC ANDERSON
Penciler

WILL BLYBERG
Inker

COMICRAFT'S JOHN ROSHELL
Lettering & Design

ALEX SINCLAIR
Colors

ALEX ROSS
Covers

BUSIEK, ANDERSON & ROSS
City Fathers

ANN
HUNTINGTON BUSIEK
Managing Editor

RICHARD STARKINGS
President & First tiger

JONATHAN PETERSON   EDITOR – ORIGINAL SERIES
JEB WOODARD   GROUP EDITOR – COLLECTED EDITIONS
LIZ ERICKSON   EDITOR – COLLECTED EDITION
JOHN ROSHELL   PUBLICATION DESIGN

SHELLY BOND   VP & EXECUTIVE EDITOR – VERTIGO

DIANE NELSON   PRESIDENT
DAN DiDIO AND JIM LEE   CO-PUBLISHERS
GEOFF JOHNS   CHIEF CREATIVE OFFICER
AMIT DESAI   SENIOR VP – MARKETING & GLOBAL FRANCHISE MANAGEMENT
NAIRI GARDINER   SENIOR VP – FINANCE
SAM ADES   VP – DIGITAL MARKETING
BOBBIE CHASE   VP – TALENT DEVELOPMENT
MARK CHIARELLO   SENIOR VP – ART, DESIGN & COLLECTED EDITIONS
JOHN CUNNINGHAM   VP – CONTENT STRATEGY
ANNE DePIES   VP – STRATEGY PLANNING & REPORTING
DON FALLETTI   VP – MANUFACTURING OPERATIONS
LAWRENCE GANEM   VP – EDITORIAL ADMINISTRATION & TALENT RELATIONS
ALISON GILL   SENIOR VP – MANUFACTURING & OPERATIONS
HANK KANALZ   SENIOR VP – EDITORIAL STRATEGY & ADMINISTRATION
JAY KOGAN   VP – LEGAL AFFAIRS
DEREK MADDALENA   SENIOR VP – SALES & BUSINESS DEVELOPMENT
DAN MIRON   VP – SALES PLANNING & TRADE DEVELOPMENT
NICK NAPOLITANO   VP – MANUFACTURING ADMINISTRATION
CAROL ROEDER   VP – MARKETING
EDDIE SCANNELL   VP – MASS ACCOUNT & DIGITAL SALES
SUSAN SHEPPARD   VP – BUSINESS AFFAIRS
COURTNEY SIMMONS   SENIOR VP – PUBLICITY & COMMUNICATIONS
JIM (SKI) SOKOLOWSKI   VP – COMIC BOOK SPECIALTY & NEWSSTAND SALES

ASTRO CITY: CONFESSION

Published by DC Comics. Compilation Copyright © 2015 Juke Box Productions. All Rights Reserved.

Originally published in single magazine form as KURT BUSIEK'S ASTRO CITY VOL. 2 4-9, WIZARD
PRESENTS ASTRO CITY ½ © 1996, 1997 Juke Box Productions. Astro City, its logos, symbols,
prominent characters featured in this volume and the distinctive likenesses thereof are trademarks of
Juke Box Productions. VERTIGO is a trademark of DC Comics. The stories, characters and incidents
featured in this publication are entirely fictional. DC Comics does not read or accept unsolicited
submissions of ideas, stories or artwork.

DC Comics, 4000 Warner Blvd., Burbank, CA 91522

A Warner Bros. Entertainment Company.

Printed by RR Donnelley, Salem, VA, USA. 8/7/15

ISBN: 978-1-4012-5830-6

Library of Congress Cataloging-in-Publication Data
Busiek, Kurt.
  Astro City : confession / Kurt Busiek, writer ; Brent Anderson,
artist.
    pages cm
  ISBN 978-1-4012-5830-6 (hardback)
1. Graphic novels. I. Anderson, Brent Eric, illustrator. II. Title.
PN6728.A79B73 2015
741.5'973--dc23
          2015012171

PEFC Certified

Printed on paper from
sustainably managed
forests and controlled
sources

www.pefc.org

PEFC/29-31-75

TO MY PARENTS, SYDNEY KIRK THOMPSON KENNEDY AND DON KURT BUSIEK, FOR... WELL, FOR EVERYTHING.
— *Kurt*

TO THE CITY OF NEW YORK — HAD IT CONTAINED SUPERHEROES, I WOULD HAVE SEEN THEM. AND TO MY FATHER, DON GOLDEN ANDERSON, WHO MIGHT HAVE BEEN ONE HAD I BUT LOOKED.
— *Brent*

TO KURT'S PARENTS. GOD BLESS THEM FOR CREATING SUCH A WONDERFUL CHILD.
— *Alex*

CONTENTS

LISTEN, NOW. READ THIS CAREFULLY, because I am going to tell you something important. More than that: I am about to tell you one of the secrets of the trade. I mean it. This is the magic trick upon which all good fiction depends: it's the angled mirror in the box behind which the doves are hidden, the hidden compartment beneath the table.

It's this:

*There is room for things to mean
more than they literally mean.*

That was it.

Doesn't seem that important to you? Not impressed? Convinced you could get deeper, sager advice about writing from a fortune cookie? Trust me. I just told you something important. We'll come back to it.

THERE ARE, IN MY OPINION, TWO MAJOR WAYS in which superheroes are used in popular fiction. In the first way superheroes mean, purely and simply, what they mean on the surface. In the second kind of fiction, they mean what they mean on the surface, true, but they also mean more than that — they mean pop culture on the one hand, and hopes and dreams, or the converse of hopes and dreams, a falling away of innocence, on the other.

The lineage of superheroes goes way back: it starts, obviously, in the 1930s, and then goes back into the depths of the newspaper strip, and then into literature, co-opting Sherlock Holmes, Beowulf and various heroes and gods along the way.

Robert Mayer's novel *Superfolks* used superheroes as a metaphor for all that America had become in the 1970s: the loss of the American dream meant the loss of American dreams, and vice versa.

Joseph Torchia took the iconography of Superman and wrote *The Kryptonite Kid,* a powerful and beautiful epistolary novel about a kid who believes, literally, in Superman, and who, in a book constructed as a series of letters to Superman, has to come to terms with his life and his heart.

IN THE 1980S, FOR THE FIRST TIME, WRITERS BEGAN WRITING comics superheroes in which the characters were as much commentary upon superheroes as they were superheroes: Alan Moore led the way in this, as did Frank Miller.

One of the elements that fused back into comics at that time was the treatment of some comics themes in prose fiction: *Superfolks* and *The Kryptonite Kid*, short stories such as Norman Spinrad's "It's a Bird, It's a Plane...," essays like Larry Niven's (literally) seminal "Man of Steel, Woman of Kleenex."

The resurgence that hit comics at this time also surfaced in prose fiction — the early volumes of the George R.R. Martin-edited *Wild Cards* anthologies did a fine job of reinvoking the joy of superheroes in a prose context.

The problem with the mid-80s revival of interesting superheroes was that the wrong riffs were the easiest to steal. *Watchmen* and *The Dark Knight Returns* spawned too many bad comics: humourless, grey, violent and dull. When the *Wild Cards* anthologies were turned into comics everything that made them interesting as commentaries upon comics evaporated, too.

So after the first Moore, Miller and Martin-led flush of superheroes (they weren't deconstructed. Just, briefly, respected), things returned, more or less, to the status quo, and a pendulum swing gave us, in the early 90s, superhero comics which were practically contentless: poorly written, and utterly literal. There was even one publisher who trumpeted four issues of good writers as the ultimate marketing gimmick — every bit as good as foil-embossed covers.

There is room to move beyond the literal. Things can mean more than they mean. It's why *Catch-22* isn't just about fighter pilots in the second world war. It's why "I Have No Mouth, And I Must Scream" is about more than a bunch of people trapped inside a supercomputer. It's why *Moby Dick* is about (believe fifty thousand despairing college professors or not, but it's still true) a lot more than whaling.

And I'm not talking about allegory, here, or metaphor, or even The Message. I'm talking about what the story is about, and then I'm talking about what it's *about*.

Things can mean more than they literally mean. And that's the dividing line between art and everything that isn't art. Or one of the lines, anyway.

CURRENTLY, SUPERHERO FICTIONS SEEM TO BREAK INTO TWO kinds: there are the workaday, more or less pulp fictions which are turned out by the yard by people who are trying their hardest, or not. And then there are the other kind, and there are precious few of them.

There are two obvious current exceptions — Alan Moore's *Supreme*, an exercise in rewriting fifty years of Superman into something that means something.

And then — and some of you might have thought that I might have forgotten it, given how far we've got into this introduction without it being mentioned, there is *Astro City*. Which traces its lineage back in two directions — into the world of classic superhero archetypes, but equally into the world of *The Kryptonite Kid*, a world in which all this stuff, this dumb wonderful four-colour stuff has real emotional weight and depth, and it means more than it literally means.

And that is the genius and the joy of *Astro City*.

*M*E? I'M JADED, WHERE SUPERHEROES ARE CONCERNED. Jaded and tired and fairly burnt out, if truth be told. Not utterly burned out, though. I thought I was, until, a couple of years ago, I found myself in a car with Kurt Busiek, and his delightful wife Ann. (We were driving to see Scott McCloud and his wife Ivy, and their little girl Sky, and it was a very memorable and eventful evening, ending as it did in the unexpected birth of Scott and Ivy's daughter Winter.) And in the car, on the way, we started talking about Batman.

Pretty soon Kurt and I were co-plotting a complete Batman story; and not just a Batman story, but the coolest, strangest Batman story you can imagine, in which every relationship in the world of Batman was turned inside out and upside down, and, in the finest comic book tradition, everything you thought you knew turned out to be a lie.

We were doing this for fun. I doubt that either of us will ever do anything with the story. We were just enjoying ourselves.

But, for several hours, I found myself caring utterly and deeply about Batman. Which is, I suspect, part of Kurt Busiek's special talent. If I were writing a different kind of introduction, I might call it a super power.

Astro City is what would have happened if those old comics, with their fine simplicities and their primal, four-colour characters, had been *about* something. Or rather, it assumes they *were* about something, and tells you the tales that, on the whole, slipped through the cracks.

It's a place inspired by the worlds and worldviews of Stan Lee and Jack Kirby, of Gardner Fox and John Broome, of Jerry Seigel and Bob Finger and the rest of them; a city where anything can happen: in the story that follows we have (and I'm trying hard not to give too much away) a crimefighter bar, a serial killing, an alien invasion, a crackdown on costumed heroes, a hero's mysterious secret... all of them the happy pulp elements of a thousand comics-by-the-yard.

Except that, here, as in the rest of *Astro City*, Kurt Busiek manages to take all of these elements and let them mean more than they literally mean.

(Again, I am not talking about allegory here. I'm talking story, and what makes some stories magic while others just sit there, lifeless and dull.)

*A*STRO CITY: CONFESSION IS A COMING OF age story, in which a young man learns a lesson. (Robert A. Heinlein claimed in an essay in the 1940s, published in Lloyd Esbach's collection of SF writer essays *Of Worlds Beyond*, that there are only three stories, which we tell over and over again. He said he had thought there were only two, "Boy Meets Girl" and "The Little Tailor," until L. Ron Hubbard pointed out to him that there was also "A Man Learns A Lesson." And, Heinlein maintained, if you add in their opposites — someone fails to learn a lesson, two people don't fall in love, and so on — you may have all the stories there are. But then, we can move beyond the literal.) It's a growing up story, set in the city in Kurt's mind.

One of the things I like about *Astro City* is that Kurt Busiek lists all of his collaborators on the front cover. He knows how important each of them is to the final outcome: each element does what it is meant to, and each of them gives their best and a little more: Alex Ross's covers ground each issue in a photoreal sort of hyper-reality; Brent Anderson's pencils and Will Blyberg's inks are perfectly crafted, always wisely at the service of the story, never obtrusive, always convincing. The colouring by Alex Sinclair, and the Comicraft lettering by John Roshell are both slick, and, in the best sense of the word, inconspicuous.

Astro City, in the hands of Kurt Busiek and his collaborators, is art, and it is good art. It recognizes the strengths of the four-colour heroes, and it creates something — a place, perhaps, or a medium, or just a tone of voice — in which good stories are told. There is room for things to mean more than they literally mean, and this is certainly true in Astro City.

I look forward to being able to visit it for a very long time to come.

Neil Gaiman
26 October 1997
ROME.

NEIL GAIMAN USED TO HAVE MORE EISNER AWARDS THAN ANYONE ELSE, BUT HE SUSPECTS THAT ALAN MOORE, KURT BUSIEK OR JAMES ROBINSON MUST HAVE CAUGHT UP BY NOW. HIS MOST RECENT WORKS ARE *STARDUST*, A FOUR-PART SHORT NOVEL ILLUSTRATED BY CHARLES VESS, *NEVERWHERE*, A LONGER NOVEL ILLUSTRATED ONLY BY THE POWER OF THE IMAGINATION, AND *BEOWULF*, A RE-TELLING OF THE ORIGINAL SAGA WHICH HE WROTE WITH FILM-MAKER ROGER AVARY, AND WHICH GOES INTO PRODUCTION IN 1998. UNLESS IT DOESN'T, THIS BEING HOLLYWOOD, AFTER ALL.

CHAPTER 1

I LEFT BUCHANAN CORNERS IN EARLY SUMMER. IT WAS ALREADY *HOT*...

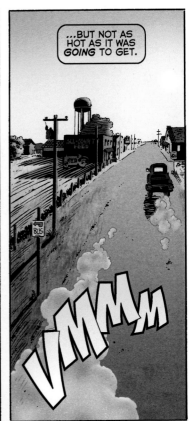

...BUT NOT AS HOT AS IT WAS *GOING* TO GET.

VMMM

I'M *SORRY*, DAD. I KNOW I SHOULD HAVE FINISHED *SCHOOL*, BUT I JUST COULDN'T *STAND* IT ANY MORE. THE LOOKS, THE SMIRKS...

I FELT LIKE I WAS *DESERTING* YOU --

-- BUT AFTER THE WAY *YOU* --

OH, IT DOESN'T *MATTER*.

I JUST HAD TO GET *OUT*. I HAD TO STOP BEING "THE KINNEY BOY," AND FIND SOMEPLACE I COULD BE *SOMEONE ELSE*.

AND I *DID*.

AND WAKING UP ON THAT BUS, IN THE *MORNING LIGHT* --

THERE IT *IS*.

-- IT WAS LIKE A *DREAM.*

I WAS THERE. I WAS REALLY *THERE.*

SEEING THE BUILDINGS RISING UP AROUND ME, HIGHER AND HIGHER...

CROSSING THE *OUTCAULT* BRIDGE...

I WAS REALLY *THERE.* BREATHING THE AIR SEEING IT ALL, BEING IN A PLACE I'D ONLY *READ* ABOUT BEFORE.

I'LL TELL YOU, THE FIRST THING I DID --

-- WAS LOOK AROUND TO SEE IF I COULD SPOT ANY OF *THEM.*

AND WOULDN'T YOU *KNOW* IT...

THERE! BY THE STATION! THAT'S --

YEAH. IT'S THE *JESUS FREAKS.* AGAIN.

WHY CAN'T THEY PICK SOME *OTHER* CORNER, JUST ONCE? JUST ONCE? A DIFFERENT TIME OF *DAY?*

I AM SO SICK OF THOSE *JERKS...*

I DIDN'T KNOW WHAT HE WAS *TALKING* ABOUT. THEY WERE SUPERHEROES. REAL, LIVE *SUPERHEROES* --

16

I MEAN, SO THEY'RE RELIGIOUS. WHAT DIFFERENCE DID THAT --

HAVE YOU BEEN *SAVED*?

H-*HUH*?

HAVE YOU ACCEPTED *JESUS CHRIST* AS YOUR PERSONAL *SAVIOR*?

ARE YOU PREPARED TO BE *JUDGED* BY YOUR *MAKER*?

UH, NOT *TODAY*...

I, *UH* -- LOOK, I'M NOT MUCH OF A *CHURCH-GOER* --

TAKE A *PAMPHLET.* READ THE *WORD.*

HEY, LAFCADIO! BACK *OFF*, WILLYA -- -- CAN'T YOU SEE YOU'RE *UNNERVIN'* THE KID?

HUH?

IT'S THE *EYES*, KID. LOOKS LIKE HE'S GONNA *EATCHA*, DON'T HE?

WELL, DON'T WORRY. THE J.F.'S ARE *ANNOYIN'*, BUT THEY'RE *HARMLESS* -- 'LESS YOU'RE ALLERGIC TO *PSALMS* AN' *PREACHIN'*! STILL, YOU WANNA *WATCH* YOURSELF --

-- THERE'S WORSE'N *THEM* AROUND, AN' YOU DON'T WANNA LET YOUR *GUARD* DOWN. IT'S A *BIG CITY*, REMEMBER?

UH, *THANKS*, I'LL TRY TO --

BUT THEN, I HAD A *LOT* TO GET USED TO.

-- *THIRD BODY* FOUND IN FASS GARDENS, ON THE OUTSKIRTS OF *SHADOW HILL.*

THE BODY, AN UNIDENTIFIED *BLACK MALE* IN HIS MID-FORTIES, IS APPARENTLY THAT OF A *TRANSIENT.*

POLICE CONFIRM THAT THE BODY HAS BEEN MUTILATED, BUT ARE WITHHOLDING THE DETAILS WHILE THE INVESTIGATION IS ACTIVE.

IN OTHER NEWS, *SAMARITAN* WAS HONORED BY THE ASTRO CITY METROPOLITAN COUNCIL OF SCHOOLS TODAY --

-- FOR HIS RESCUE OF A SCHOOL BUS FULL OF *THIRD GRADERS* LAST MONTH. THE BANQUET, WHICH WAS HELD AT --

IT WAS SUCH A *BIG* PLACE.

I FELT *TINY* THERE, SURROUNDED BY MILES OF CONCRETE AND SHADOWS, BY MILLIONS OF *STRANGERS.*

I DIDN'T *KNOW* ANYONE. I DIDN'T EVEN KNOW WHAT'S AROUND THE *CORNER.* IT WAS ALL... OVERPOWERING.

BUT I COULD GET *USED* TO IT. I KNEW THAT. IT WAS JUST A LITTLE SCARY BECAUSE IT WASN'T *FAMILIAR* YET. BUT IT *WOULD* BE.

I WAS THERE. THAT'S WHAT *COUNTED.*

I WAS *THERE.*

THE NEXT DAY, I STARTED TO GET TO KNOW THE *CITY.*

IT'S DIFFERENT, *LOOKING* AT STREETS AND BUILDINGS, THAN IT IS READING ABOUT THEM IN *GUIDEBOOKS.*

SO I LOOKED AT THEM. AND I GOT A *FEEL* FOR THEM. AND MORE AND MORE, AS I WANDERED AROUND --

-- I FOUND MYSELF LOOKING TO THE *SKY.*

YOU MUST BE FROM *OUT OF TOWN.*

HUH?

WE DON'T *SEE* THEM EVERY DAY. THEY'RE AROUND, SURE, BUT IT'S JUST *SOMETIMES* YOU SEE THEM.

WAS I *THAT* OBVIOUS?

A LITTLE, MAYBE. BUT IT WEARS OFF. I'VE BEEN HERE TEN YEARS, AND MOST OF THE TIME, THIS COULD BE *ANY* ORDINARY --

-- OH, *LOOK!*

IT'S THE *FIRST FAMILY* -- IN A TEARING HURRY! I WONDER WHERE THEY'RE *GOING* --?

SODAS   FOOT LONGS

YEAH, IT *WORE OFF.*

YOU COULD *TELL...*

IT WAS A COUPLE OF *WEEKS* BEFORE I FOUND THE PLACE I WAS LOOKING FOR. I'D READ ABOUT IT IN JOHNNY CRASH'S *MEMOIRS.*

IT WAS IN A CRUDDY, *DANGEROUS* NEIGHBORHOOD -- BUT I GUESS THAT GAVE THEM THE *PRIVACY* THEY WANTED.

NOBODY BOTHERED *ME,* THOUGH. MAYBE THEY COULD TELL THAT I KNEW HOW TO TAKE *CARE* OF MYSELF.

MAYBE IT WAS IN THE WAY I *WALKED,* OR SOMETHING.

I *HOPED* SO, ANYWAY. FIVE YEARS OF BIKING TWENTY MILES TO THE ONLY DOJO IN HOOD COUNTY OUGHT TO COUNT FOR *SOMETHING.*

ch-LING

WE'RE NOT *OPEN* YET.

UH -- I'M HERE ABOUT THE *JOB?*

THERE WAS AN *AD* IN THE PAPER?

YEAH? YOU WASHED *DISHES* BEFORE? BUSSED TABLES? YOU FAST ON YOUR *FEET?*

YOU CAN GET OUT OF THE WAY IF *TROUBLE* STARTS?

YES, YES, I LIKE TO *THINK* SO -- AND *TRY* ME.

FINE. YOU'RE *UNDERAGE,* KID, BUT I WON'T KICK IF YOU DON'T. FILL OUT THE PAPERWORK OVER THERE. WE OPEN IN AN *HOUR.*

HE WAS *K.O. CARSON* -- HE'D BEEN THE *BLACK BADGE* UNTIL 1972, WHEN HE RETIRED AND OPENED THIS PLACE.

22

24

-- BUT *RESPECT?* HE HAD THAT IN *SPADES.*

SOMEDAY.

SOMEDAY.

YOU DIDN'T ASK FOR ANY *AUTOGRAPHS.* YOU DIDN'T BRING A *CAMERA* AND TAKE PICTURES.

HUH? NO, OF COURSE NOT. WHY *WOULD* I?

THE THING IS, KID, YOU'RE TOO *SMART* TO BE BUSSIN' TABLES AN' SCHLEPPIN' POPCORN IN A *BEER JOINT.*

IF YOU'RE NOT HERE FOR *SOUVENIRS,* OR FOR A *NEWS* STORY, THEN YOU MUST BE HERE FOR *ANOTHER* REASON.

HEY, LOOK, I --

DON'T WORRY, I'M NOT GOING TO TRY TO TALK YOU *OUT* OF IT.

BUT YOU'RE IN THE WRONG *PLACE.* THESE AREN'T THE RIGHT KIND OF *COSTUMES.*

HERE, TAKE *THIS.* TELL 'EM *I* SENT YOU OVER. I DON'T KNOW IF THEY HAVE ANY *OPENINGS,* BUT...

BUTLER'S
BY INVITATION ONLY
34 Wodehouse Mews
Astro City,

WHAT...?

NOW *THIS*, I HADN'T SEEN IN ANY ARTICLE, BIOGRAPHY, OR MEMOIR. *ANYWHERE.*

I DID SOME *RESEARCH* ON IT IN THE ASTRO CITY PUBLIC LIBRARY, THOUGH. IT WAS A *PRIVATE CLUB*, NEAR MUSEUM ROW.

THE OWNER WAS A *JEDSON GODFREY*. HE'D INHERITED IT FROM *ANDERS VON RUPERT*, THE THIRD-GENERATION COPPER MILLIONAIRE, WHOM HE'D BEEN *BUTLER* FOR UP UNTIL VAN RUPERT'S *DEATH*.

N° 34

IT WAS RUMORED THAT VAN RUPERT HAD BEEN *LEOPARDMAN*, BUT NOTHING HAD EVER BEEN PROVEN, AND GODFREY WASN'T *TALKING*.

FROM WHAT I COULD TELL, BUTLER'S WAS *VERY* EXCLUSIVE. NO *MEMBERSHIP* LISTS, NO PUBLICLY-LISTED *EVENTS.*

JUST A LITTLE *OWNERSHIP* INFORMATION AND SOME *LICENSES.*

K.O. TOLD ME THEY HAD AN *EMPATH* THERE -- THAT IF I WASN'T TRUSTWORTHY, I WOULDN'T GET *IN* --

-- AND MIGHT NOT EVEN REMEMBER GOING *THERE.*

MAYBE HE WASN'T TELLING THE TRUTH, JUST TRYING TO MAKE SURE I TOOK IT *SERIOUSLY.* IF SO, IT SURE *WORKED.*

WELL...

...HERE GOES NOTHING.

GOOD AFTERNOON. YOU COME *HIGHLY* RECOMMENDED. WE *DO* HAVE AN OPENING FOR A BUSBOY, IF YOU'D *CARE* FOR IT.

THE SHIFT RUNS FIVE IN THE AFTERNOON UNTIL ONE IN THE *MORNING.* FOUR DAYS A *WEEK,* TO START.

WE PAY *TRIPLE* MINIMUM WAGE, AND A *HANDSOME* BENEFITS PACKAGE. MISS *KENNEALY* WILL GO OVER IT WITH YOU.

WE EXPECT PROMPTNESS, DILIGENCE AND *CIRCUMSPECTION.* THIS IS A PRIVATE CLUB. IS THAT *ACCEPTABLE* TO YOU?

UH -- YES. IT SOUNDS *GREAT!*

HOW *NICE.* HERE'S YOUR *MASK.*

MASK? WE, UH, WEAR *MASKS?*

DO YOU HAVE A *PROBLEM* WITH MASKS?

NO -- NO, OF *COURSE* NOT. NOT AT ALL.

I'M SO RELIEVED TO *HEAR* IT. YOU'LL FIND MISS KENNEALY'S OFFICE JUST OFF THE *BAR.*

I DIDN'T HAVE TO LOOK TO KNOW THE OTHER BUSBOYS WERE *EYEING* ME AS I PASSED THE KITCHEN.

I COULD *FEEL* IT. TO THEM, I WAS AN *INTRUDER* -- A POTENTIAL *THREAT.*

MAYBE THAT'D *CHANGE* ONCE I'D BEEN THERE A WHILE. MAYBE IT *WOULDN'T.* I DIDN'T CARE.

I WAS *USED* TO IT.

I JUST DID MY *JOB.* MR. GODFREY WANTED PROMPTNESS, DILIGENCE AND CIRCUMSPECTION?

HE'D *GET* IT.

IT WAS A DIFFERENT CROWD FROM THE ONE AT *BRUISER'S.*

A *VERY* DIFFERENT CROWD.

I TRIED NOT TO *STARE,* BUT I COULDN'T HELP BUT WONDER. THESE *SMILING* MEN -- THESE *ATHLETIC* WOMEN --

-- WERE THEY *REALLY* --

HEY, THERE, BOYS AND GIRLS! DON'T LOOK *NOW* --

-- WHEN --

EVERYBODY REACTED SO FAST --

-- BUT --

FREEZE!

I MEAN IT! ANYONE MOVES A *MUSCLE* --

-- AND THE *KID* HERE GETS A SKULL FULL OF *EPOXY!*

THAT'S BETTER.

YOU THOUGHT YOU COULD JUST THROW ME IN JAIL AND *FORGET* ME, DIDN'T YOU? YOU THOUGHT I WAS JUST SOME *JOKE.*

-- SOMEONE *ANYBODY* COULD BEAT. WELL, I *FOUND* YOUR LITTLE HIDEAWAY, AND I CAUGHT YOU ALL *FLAT-FOOTED* --

-- AND NOW, **GLUE-GUN'S** GOING TO MAKE YOU ALL *PAY!*

AT FIRST, I FELT *HUMILIATED,* EMBARRASSED BY THE LAUGHTER. I FELT LIKE I'D DONE THE WRONG THING, *OVERREACTED* SOMEHOW --

-- UNTIL --

SEE THAT?

ONE KICK

WAKES UP, HE'LL BE SO

A LOSER, ALWAYS A LOSER

LED HIM HERE?

HAD TO BE CRACKERJACK

KID MOVED

NO HESITATION

SAW THE OPENING

COLD LINGUINI, RIGHT IN THE

COULDN'T HAVE DONE THAT AT THAT AGE

-- I REALIZED THEY WEREN'T LAUGHING *AT ME.*

THEY ACTUALLY THOUGHT I DID *GOOD.*

I TRIED TO HIDE MY SMILE BY STAYING *BUSY* --

I'LL JUST GET *THESE* --

WHY DON'T YOU *LEAVE* THOSE --

-- LET SOMEONE *ELSE* CLEAN UP? YOU'VE *EARNED* IT.

NICE *JOB* THERE, KID. YOU'LL GO *FAR.*

I WAS *FLOATING* ON THAT THE REST OF THE NIGHT --

-- AND WHEN MY SHIFT *ENDED*, I JUST KNEW I WASN'T GOING TO GET ANY SLEEP FOR THE REST OF THE *NIGHT*.

HEY, *KINNEY.*

AND I WAS RIGHT.

WHAT -- ?

I WAS JUST WRONG ABOUT THE *REASON*, THAT'S ALL.

I BEEN HERE TWO YEARS. TWO *YEARS!*

BENNY'S BEEN HERE *EIGHTEEN MONTHS.* SANDY, JIM, RACHEL, WE'VE ALL PUT IN OUR TIME. PAID OUR *DUES.*

AND YOU'RE HERE, WHAT, THREE *DAYS?* AND YOU GET *THAT?*

THAT SHOULD HAVE BEEN ONE OF *US.* THAT SHOULD HAVE BEEN *OUR* CHANCE.

HUH? I JUST DID WHAT --

SAVE IT! YOU THINK WE DON'T KNOW WHY YOU'RE HERE? YOU THINK ANY OF US DON'T WANT THE SAME THING?

YOU STOLE OUR CHANCE, IS WHAT YOU DID --

-- AND WE'RE TAKING IT OUT OF YOUR --

BACK OFF!

I STOLE YOUR CHANCE? IS THERE A SIGN-UP SHEET OR SOMETHING?

"EXCUSE ME, GLUE-GUN -- COULD ONE OF THE SENIOR BUSBOYS SUBSTITUTE FOR ME? HE WANTS TO IMPRESS THE CUSTOMERS."

I JUST REACTED TO WHAT HAPPENED. YOU HAVE A PROBLEM WITH THAT? LET'S GO.

THERE WERE SEVEN OF THEM, AND ONE OF ME. I FIGURED I WAS GOING DOWN, BUT I WASN'T GOING TO GO ALONE.

EXCUSE ME.

37

CHAPTER

MY DAD USED TO SAY *A LOT* OF THINGS, THOUGH. I USED TO THINK HE WAS THE *SMARTEST* MAN IN THE WORLD.

BUT HE *DIED*, IN A SMALL TOWN IN THE MIDDLE OF NOWHERE, SURROUNDED BY PEOPLE WHO USED HIM AND *BELITTLED* HIM --

AND *ME* --

WHAK

UHH!

-- I DID WHAT HE *NEVER* DID.

I WENT TO THE CITY -- *ASTRO CITY.* I WENT LOOKING TO *MAKE* SOMETHING OF MYSELF.

GET HI-- FF!

KRAK

HAKHH!

AND I WORKED *HARD*, AND I LOOKED FOR A WAY INTO THE WORLD I WANTED TO BE A PART OF.

AND IN LESS TIME THAN I'D *EXPECTED* --

43

KRAK

BEHIND YOU. ALWAYS KEEP A SENSE OF WHERE *EVERYONE* IS. FOCUS IN ONE DIRECTION, AND YOU'LL *LOSE.*

UH, *THANKS!* I'LL REMEMBER THAT NEXT --

--TIIII --!

BRAAADDAAT

AH-*AH,* TUGLIEWSKI.

BAD *MANNERS.*

WHAK

HUH? HOW DID YOU -- ?!

THE COSTUME WORKED OUT *WELL?* THE WEIGHTED HEM OF THE SURPLICE KEPT IT OUT OF YOUR *WAY?*

AND THE LOW-FRICTION COATING KEPT THEM FROM *GRABBING* YOU BY IT?

UH, YEAH, I *GUESS.* BUT HOW --

44

-- AMBASSADOR WAS RESCUED AND THE *PYRAMID* ASSAULT TEAM CAPTURED BY *HONOR GUARD,* AFTER A PITCHED BATTLE.

WITNESSES STATE THAT IF NOT FOR HONOR GUARD'S INTERVENTION, HALF OF THE *SECURITY COUNCIL* WOULD HAVE BEEN *WIPED OUT.*

BUT LOCALLY, SUPERHERO APPROVAL RATINGS HAVE TAKEN A *DIP* --

-- AMID REPORTS OF *CRACKERJACK* ROBBING THE FASS GARDENS BRANCH OF ASTROBANK --

-- AND *WINGED VICTORY* DENOUNCING THE CITY'S CATHOLIC SCHOOLS, INSISTING THAT THEIR TEACHINGS ARE "HARMFUL MYSTICAL RUBBISH."

COMMUNITY LEADERS MET WITH THE MAYOR THIS MORNING TO DISCUSS --

I WATCHED THE NEWS, AND THE DETAILS DIDN'T *MATTER.*

THERE WAS ALWAYS A HERO OR TWO ON THE OUTS WITH THE *PUBLIC,* AND IT USUALLY TURNED OUT TO BE NOTHING.

WHAT WAS *IMPORTANT* -- AT LEAST TO ME -- WAS THAT I LOOKED AT THOSE IMAGES AND I THOUGHT OF THEM AS "*US.*"

I WAS *ONE* OF THEM.

I HAD A SECRET FROM THE PEOPLE AROUND ME. I WAS SOMETHING SPECIAL.

AND I COULDN'T RESIST --

THERE WERE PARTS OF IT THAT WERE *CLOSED* TO THE PUBLIC. NEVER FINISHED, NEVER CONSECRATED, FALLEN INTO *DISREPAIR.*

AND EVERY NIGHT, IN ONE OBSCURE *VESTRY,* GUARDED BY RUSTY PADLOCKS AND TOPPLED STONE --

-- I UNDERWENT MY *TRAINING.*

NO.

IT IS NOT ENOUGH TO MERELY *PARRY* THE BLOW. YOU MUST ALSO SET YOUR OPPONENT UP FOR THE *COUNTER-STRIKE...*

SEAN *HANRAHAN.* THE ORIGINAL QUEEN'S BISHOP IN THE *CHESSMEN,* LATER ONE OF *HEADSTONE'S* LIEUTENANTS.

WENT AWAY IN *'87* FOR RACKETEERING, KIDNAPPING AND CONSPIRACY TO COMMIT. PAROLED IN APRIL *'92.*

GOOD.

NOW LET'S SEE YOU *RUN* THEM, SEE IF YOU CAN FIND A *MATCH.*

RULES AND *FACTS* AND *FORMULAS,* OVER AND OVER. EXCEPT *SOME* NIGHTS -- MAYBE THREE OR FOUR TIMES A WEEK --

ENOUGH STUDY. LET'S GO *OUT.*

-- SOME NIGHTS WE WENT OUT AND MADE IT *REAL.*

-- BUT AT LEAST I FELT LIKE AN IDIOT WITH *POTENTIAL*.

AFTER ALL, HE DIDN'T *HAVE* TO TRAIN ME.

HE'D ARRANGED FOR ME TO STAY IN ONE OF THE DORMS AT *ROBINSON PREP*, UP NEAR MUSEUM ROW --

-- AND TO TAKE CLASSES THERE ONCE THE *FALL TERM* STARTED.

SPRANG HOUSE

HE DIDN'T HAVE TO DO *ANY* OF THAT --

-- NOT UNLESS HE THOUGHT IT WAS *WORTH* DOING.

HEY, *KINNEY!* IT'S TWO IN THE AFTERNOON -- YOU GONNA SLEEP THE WHOLE *DAY* AWAY?

HUH?

OH, HI, CHET. 'SUP?

WE'RE HEADED DOWN TO *MOONEY'S* FOR A SLICE. YOU UP TO COME *WITH?*

SURE, SURE. LET ME JUST THROW SOME *CLOTHES* ON --

-- I'LL CATCH UP TO YOU, OKAY?

I COULDN'T HELP BUT *WONDER* -- I NEVER SAW THE CONFESSOR DURING THE DAY. HE HADN'T TOLD ME WHO HE REALLY *WAS*, AND I HADN'T ASKED -- BUT --

-- WAS HE *AROUND?* WAS HE... SOMEWHERE *HERE?*

51

EVEN DURING SUMMER BREAK, ROBINSON HAD LOTS OF *ADULTS* AROUND --

-- *PROFESSORS* GETTING READY FOR NEXT TERM, *ADMINISTRATORS, GROUNDSMEN* --

-- AND THE CONFESSOR HAD A *SCHOLARLY* MANNER --

HE COULD BE RIGHT *HERE.* I COULD WALK RIGHT PAST HIM AND NOT *KNOW* IT.

-- *FIFTH BODY DISCOVERED, IN WHAT'S COMING TO BE CALLED THE "SHADOW HILL MURDERS."*

POLICE SOURCES SAY THE BODY, AS YET UNIDENTIFIED, WAS RITUALLY MUTILATED, AND THAT CULT ACTIVITY COULD NOT BE RULED OUT.

IN OTHER NEWS, THE ADVENTURER CALLED *CRACKERJACK* WAS AGAIN THE SUBJECT OF CRIMINAL ALLEGATIONS TODAY, AS --

GEEZ -- *MUTILATED!* CAN YOU *BELIEVE* IT?

ALL THAT ABOUT MONSTERS AND *MAGIC* AND STUFF -- I WOULDN'T GO UP TO SHADOW HILL IF YOU *PAID ME!*

BUT PEOPLE LIVE THERE -- *THOUSANDS* OF 'EM. AND STEVE McANN, HE SPENT A *NIGHT* UP THERE, ON A BET --

-- AND *HE* CAME OUT OKAY.

WHAT ABOUT YOU, BRIAN. WOULD *YOU* GO UP TO SHADOW HILL?

WELL, I --

HEY THERE, EVERYBODY!

TAKE A LOOK -- THE NEW ISSUE OF *CURRENT*.

PICTURES OF *ALTAR BOY*.

ALTAR BOY? THE NEW GUY WHO'S HANGING AROUND WITH THE *CONFESSOR*?

COOL.

Altar Boy, newest crime-fighter in Astro City, caught in the act of apprehending

YOU NOTICE THEY NEVER GET ANY PICTURES OF THE CONFESSOR *HIMSELF*. I SAW AN *'ARTIST'S RENDERING'* ONCE, BUT THAT'S IT.

YEAH, HE STAYS OUT'VE THE *LIMELIGHT*. I GUESS HE HASN'T TAUGHT THE KID HOW TO *DO* THAT YET...

HE LOOKS LIKE HE'S ABOUT OUR AGE. MAN, THAT MUST BE *GREAT*.

SURE, BUT *"ALTAR BOY"*? IT'S A PRETTY DUMB *NAME*, DON'T YOU THINK?

WHO CARES? I THINK HE'S *CUTE*.

LOOK AT THAT *SMILE*...

YOU THINK HE'S CUTE? REALLY?

ADMIRING YOURSELF?

GAHH!

YOU STARTLED THE *HELL* OUT OF ME!

YOU WEREN'T PAYING *ATTENTION.* COME ON --

-- LET'S GO *OUT.*

KLUD

WRAK

KRAK

YOU KNOW, I WAS *THINKING.* WHY DON'T WE GO AFTER WHOEVER'S KILLING THOSE PEOPLE IN *SHADOW HILL?*

SHADOW HILL? YOU WANT TO SOLVE THE *SHADOW HILL* MURDERS?

WELL, WHY *NOT?* IS THERE SOME REASON WE *AVOID* SHADOW HILL?

SHADOW HILL HAS ITS OWN *PROTECTORS*. AND ITS OWN MEANS OF DEALING WITH *PREDATORS*.

YOU WANT TO TAKE *CARE* -- OVERCONFIDENCE CAN LEAD YOU INTO WORSE TRAPS THAN --

WHOA, *WHOA*, HOLD IT!

THIS IS WHERE YOU GIVE ME SOME *CRYPTIC LESSON* AND THEN *VANISH*, LEAVING ME TALKING INTO THIN AIR.

WHY DO YOU ACT SO *STRANGE? WHERE* DO YOU *GO?* WHO *ARE* YOU WHEN YOU'RE NOT THE CONFESSOR?

OH, IS *THAT* HOW IT'S DONE?

I MUST HAVE BEEN *CONFUSED*. I THOUGHT WE WERE DETECTIVES. I THOUGHT WE *INVESTIGATED* AND *DISCOVERED* THINGS.

IMAGINE MY *SURPRISE*. ALL WE NEEDED TO DO WAS *ASK* THE DEACON TO TELL US HIS CRIMINAL PLANS.

WE'LL JUST *ASK* THE GUILLOTEAM WHERE THEY'LL STRIKE NEXT.

I DIDN'T MEAN --

YOU WANT TO KNOW WHO I *AM*, BOY?

AND LIKE *THAT* --

YOU WANT TO KNOW MY *SECRETS?* WHERE I *GO?* WHERE I *CAME* FROM?

EARN YOUR ANSWERS, BOY. FIND OUT FOR *YOURSELF*.

THEN WE'LL TALK.

-- HE WAS GONE. *AGAIN.*

AND THE WORST PART ABOUT IT WAS THAT HE WAS *RIGHT.*

HE'D BEEN TRAINING ME TO *INVESTIGATE.* TO LEARN. TO LOOK AT THE *PATTERNS* AND SEE WHAT DIDN'T *FIT.*

BUT WITH HIM -- I DIDN'T EVEN KNOW WHERE TO *START.* I COULDN'T SEE THE PATTERN AT *ALL.*

I LOOKED AT EVERY MAN I SAW OVER *SIX FEET* TALL AND WANTED TO YANK AT THEIR FACE, JUST TO SEE IF IT WAS A *MASK.*

INSTEAD, I JUST *BURNED.* AND FELT LIKE A COMPLETE *FOOL.*

I DIDN'T GO TO THE *VESTRY* THAT NIGHT. I COULDN'T *FACE* HIM.

BUT I COULDN'T STAY *IN,* EITHER. IT WAS HOT, SWELTERING --

-- AND I HAD TO MOVE, TO WORK, TO *BURN OFF* SOME OF MY ANGER AND SHAME --

-- AND I KEPT THINKING ABOUT *FACTS* AND *PATTERNS* AND TRYING TO FIT ONE INTO THE OTHER --

-- AND THEN I *SAW* HIM.

CRACKERJACK.

HE'D BEEN A PRETTY *EFFECTIVE* SUPERHERO, EVEN IF HE WAS KINDA GIVEN TO *GRANDSTANDING*, AND THOUGHT HE WAS FUNNIER THAN *ANYONE ELSE* DID.

BUT NOW HE WAS *WANTED*, FOR ROBBERY, FOR ASSAULT, FOR OTHER THINGS, AND I COULDN'T FIGURE *OUT* --

WAIT A MINUTE.

LOOK AT THE *PATTERNS*, HE SAID. LOOK AT THE PATTERNS AND SEE WHAT DOESN'T *FIT*.

CRACKERJACK WAS A *BLOWHARD*, BUT HE WAS *HONEST*. ONE OF THE *GOOD GUYS*. AND THEN HE STARTED PULLING *CRIMES*.

SO EITHER HE'D *CHANGED* --

-- OR THE PERSON PULLING THE CRIMES WASN'T *HIM*.

AFTER THE POSSIBLITY OCCURED TO ME, IT WAS EASY TO SPOT THE GIVEAWAYS.

HIS COLORS WERE SLIGHTLY OFF, FOR ONE.

HIS SCEPTER DIDN'T WORK RIGHT, EITHER -- THE REAL ONE WRAPPED AROUND THINGS LIKE A BOLO, IT DIDN'T...GRAB THEM.

MOST PEOPLE WOULD MAYBE MISS THAT -- I'D READ A LOT ABOUT ASTRO CITY'S HEROES, AFTER ALL --

-- BUT IF THEY'D SEEN HIM SKITTERING DOWN THAT ALLEY WALL LIKE SOME GIANT INSECT, THEY'D KNOW HE WAS A FAKE.

ANYWAY, HE HEADED FOR THE MINI-MART'S FRONT DOOR --

ASTRO Mart

SUNDRIES
CIGARETTES · WE

SODAS · BEER
SNACKS · CANDY
MAGAZINES

ASTRO Mart

HOT?

BIG WICH

Only 99

BUY YOUR ASTRO CITY ROCKET HERE!

♪ TUM-TE- ♪ TUM-TUM ♪

-- AND I CHECKED AROUND FOR ANOTHER WAY IN.

ASTRO
Mart

GOOD *EVENING*, MY FINE FELLOW! BE SO KIND AS TO EMPTY THE *REGISTER*, WON'T YOU --

C-CRACKERJACK!

-- BEFORE I'M FORCED TO *BEAT YOU SENSELESS!*

SLAMM

YOU'RE NOT GOING TO BE BEATING *ANYONE*, YOU SLIMY *IMPOSTOR!*

EH -- ?

YOU'RE JUST GOING TO *TELL* ME --

-- WHO YOU *REALLY ARE!*

KRABSHH

IF I'D HAD ANY *DOUBTS* ABOUT HIM, OUR BATTLE TOOK CARE OF THEM. HE WASN'T MUCH OF A *FIGHTER* --

WHAK

BRAMM

-- AND FOCUSED ALL HIS ATTENTION ON *GETTING AWAY.*

KRAK

TROUBLE WAS --

YOU'RE *LEARNING.*

GHAH!

LEARNING? *UH,* YEAH, I GUESS I *AM.*

I LOOKED AT THE *PATTERNS,* AND I SAW THE *FLAW.* JUST LIKE YOU SAID.

HEY! HEY, WHERE'D HE *GO* -- ?!

-- AND *CRACKERJACK* MANAGED TO LOSE CUSTODY OF THE *DOPPELGANGER,* ONLY MOMENTS AFTER *CAPTURING* HIM.

THIS, AFTER APPARENTLY *WITHHOLDING* EVIDENCE FROM POLICE INVESTIGATORS FOR WEEKS -- EVIDENCE THAT COULD HAVE --

GEEZ, SHE MUST BE *PISSED* AT HAVING BOUGHT INTO THE SCAM, AND SHE'S TAKING IT OUT ON *HIM.*

YOU KNOW, HEROES LIKE HIM, AND *WINGED VICTORY* -- MAYBE IF THEY DIDN'T ACT SO *WEIRD,* THEY'D HAVE AN EASIER TIME...

OR MAYBE THEIR DIFFICULTIES WOULDN'T HAVE *ARISEN* IF THEY WEREN'T *VULNERABLE* TO THEM IN THE FIRST PLACE.

HUH?

PATTERNS. *THINK* ABOUT IT.

OKAY, *OKAY*. I GET THE *POINT*.

I'M NOT *THERE* YET. BUT I WILL BE.

SO YOU HAD CRACKERJACK PEGGED AS A *FAKE* RIGHT FROM THE *START*?

NO. IT HADN'T OCCURED TO ME AT *ALL*, ACTUALLY.

AND NOW, BACK TO THE *STUDIO*, WHERE WE'LL HAVE AN UPDATE ON THE HEAT-WAVE ON THE *HALF-HOUR* --

-- AS WELL AS MORE ON THE WINGED VICTORY *CONTROVERSY* --

"-- AND A REPORT ON THE *LATEST* BODY TO BE FOUND NEAR SHADOW HILL --"

TO BE CONTINUED

ASTRO CITY DEPT. OF PUBLIC WORKS

CHAPTER

THE MARCHES STARTED WHEN *SARA-LYNNE FELTON* DIED.

OR MORE *ACCURATELY,* I GUESS -- AFTER HER *BODY* WAS DISCOVERED.

THE GATHERING DARK

IT HAD BEEN JUST GETTING HOTTER AND *HOTTER* -- THE KIND OF DAYS WHERE NIGHTTIME BRINGS NO *RELIEF* FROM THE HEAT --

-- WHERE TEMPERS FRAY AND EVERYONE'S ON *EDGE*, WAITING FOR SOMETHING, *ANYTHING* TO BREAK --

THE *CONFESSOR* AND I WERE AFTER AN INTERNATIONALLY-WANTED CRIMINAL CALLED THE *GUNSLINGER* --

-- A PROFESSIONAL ASSASSIN WHO'D KILLED *FIVE MEN* IN AS MANY WEEKS.

-- AND NOW HE WAS IN *ASTRO CITY*.

ALTAR BOY, *STOP!* DON'T --

NO! I CAN *DO* THIS!

WE DIDN'T KNOW *WHO* HE WAS AFTER, OR *WHY* --

-- ALL WE KNEW WAS THAT HIS STRING WAS GOING TO STOP *HERE*.

THAT'S THE WAY, BOY. *THROW* YOURSELF INTO DEATH -- BE *CANNON-FODDER* FOR THE OLD MEN!

THAT'S THE WAY YOU *DO* IT IN THIS COUNTRY, ISN'T IT?

BUT WE *FOUND OUT*, AS SOON AS WE GOT BACK TO THE CATACOMBS BENEATH THE *ABANDONED VESTRY* THE CONFESSOR USED AS A BASE.

IT WAS HARD TO *MISS* IT. IT WAS ALL OVER THE NEWS.

SARA-LYNNE FELTON WAS A PRETTY, POPULAR EIGHTH-GRADER -- UNTIL SHE BECAME JUST ANOTHER NAME ON A *POLICE BLOTTER.*

WE WERE WALKING *HOME* -- SHE WANTED TO GO BUY A MAGAZINE -- THAT'S THE LAST TIME WE *SAW* HER --

IT'S A TERRIBLE THING -- A *TERRIBLE, TERRIBLE* THING -- !

IT WAS THE *SHADOW HILL KILLER.*

SHE WAS THE *EIGHTH* TO BE FOUND. THE EIGHTH KILLED, THE EIGHTH *RITUALLY MUTILATED* --

-- ALL IN THE NEIGHBORHOODS SURROUNDING SHADOW HILL. BUT SHE WAS ALSO THE *LAST STRAW.*

STOP THE KILLING

HUNDREDS OF PEOPLE TOOK TO THE STREETS. ANGRY. SCARED. DESPERATE. THEY WANTED SOMETHING *DONE* --

-- AND WHATEVER IT WAS, THEY WANTED IT DONE *NOW.* MAYBE IT WAS THE *HEAT.* MAYBE IT WAS THE *FRUSTRATION.*

MAYBE IT WAS THE FACT, AS ONE BAKERVILLE MINISTER POINTED OUT, THAT SARA-LYNNE WAS THE FIRST *WHITE* PERSON TO DIE.

BUT WHATEVER IT WAS, *I* FELT IT TOO.

WE COULD *PATROL* -- INVESTIGATE -- STAKE THE AREA *OUT* --

THERE'S GOT TO BE *SOMETHING* WE CAN DO -- !

NO.

WE AREN'T. *I'M* INVESTIGATING THIS. AS ARE OTHERS. BUT NOT *YOU* -- YOU'RE NOT *READY* YET.

AND THAT'S NOT A CUE FOR YOU TO TAKE ACTION ON YOUR *OWN.* THIS IS *SHADOW HILL.* THIS IS *BEYOND* YOUR PRESENT CAPABILITIES.

STAY *AWAY* FROM THIS. IS THAT *CLEAR?*

BUT WE CAN'T JUST *IGNORE* --

I GUESS HE WAS *RIGHT.*

IT'S NOT LIKE I COULD DO ANYTHING THE *OTHERS* WEREN'T -- ANYTHING THE OTHERS HADN'T *ALREADY* BEEN DOING.

THE CITY'S *HEROES* WERE SPENDING SO MUCH TIME PATROLLING THE BORDERS OF *SHADOW HILL* --

-- THAT CRIME WAS ACTUALLY *RISING* IN CHESLER, AND OTHER DOWNTOWN AREAS.

EVEN THE *HANGED MAN* WAS SEEN OUTSIDE THE HILL -- ROAMING, FOLLOWING SOME PATH ONLY *HE* COULD SENSE --

-- AS IF HE WAS *SNIFFING* FOR SOMETHING.

BUT NOBODY *FOUND* ANYTHING.

AND EVEN *THAT*, SOME PEOPLE FOUND SIGNIFICANT.

-- IF THEY CAN'T FIND ANYONE, MAYBE IT'S 'CAUSE HE'S HIDING IN *PLAIN SIGHT* OR SOMETHING. MAYBE IT'S ONE OF THE *HEROES.*

ONE OF THE *HEROES?* DON'T EVEN *JOKE* ABOUT IT, CHET!

WELL, WHY *NOT*, BRIAN? THEY'VE *ALL* GOT SECRETS. MAYBE -- JUST MAYBE --

-- SOME OF THOSE SECRETS AREN'T SO *HARMLESS...*

I COULDN'T STOP *THINKING* ABOUT WHAT HE'D SAID.

I DID MY *BEST* -- I PATROLLED WITH THE CONFESSOR AT NIGHT, WHEN HE WAS *AROUND* --

-- AND IN THE *DAYS*, I TRIED TO TAKE UP THE SLACK WHERE I COULD.

BUT ALL I SAW IN THE EYES AROUND ME WAS *DISAPPOINTMENT.* I'D WANTED TO *BE* SOMEBODY, AND NOW I *WAS* --

-- AND THEY EXPECTED ME TO WORK *MIRACLES.*

ONLY I DIDN'T KNOW *HOW.*

AND I COULDN'T HELP WONDERING WHERE THE CONFESSOR *WENT* IN THE DAYTIME -- AND WHY HE ACTED SO *STRANGE* SOMETIMES --

AND THEN TWO *MORE* BODIES WERE FOUND.

AND MAYOR STEVENSON CALLED A *PRESS* CONFERENCE.

-- WANT TO *THANK* YOU ALL FOR COMING.

WE ARE IN THE MIDST OF A CRISIS OF *FEAR,* AND IT HAS BECOME CLEAR THAT SWIFT, DECISIVE ACTION *MUST* BE TAKEN.

THE THREAT WE FACE IS *BEYOND* THE ABILITIES OF THE POLICE FORCE, AS CAPABLE AND DILIGENT THOUGH THEY ARE --

-- AND THE CITY'S HEROES, AS WELL, HAVE PROVEN THEMSELVES *UNEQUAL* TO THE TASK.

ACCORDINGLY --

"-- I HAVE SECURED THE SERVICES OF A *SPECIALIST.*"

HIS NAME WAS *MORDECAI CHALK.*

A PROFESSIONAL *MONSTER-HUNTER,* HE'D WORKED MOSTLY IN EUROPE. HE'D LOST AN *EYE,* AN ARM AND *MORE* TO THE CREATURES HE FOUGHT --

-- AND HAD THEM REPLACED WITH *COLD IRON* AND *SILVER.* HIS ONBOARD COMPUTER REFERENCED THOUSANDS OF VOLUMES OF *ANCIENT LORE,* THE MAYOR TOLD US --

-- AND HIS SHOTGUN FIRED SPECIALIZED CHARGES, FROM *WOLFSBANE* TO *HOLY WATER.*

CHALK GAVE A BRIEF SPEECH, PROMISING TO *STUDY* THE MATTER FOR A FEW DAYS, AND THEN BRING IN THE KILLER WITHIN A *WEEK*.

AND THEN THE MAYOR UNVEILED THE *SECOND* PART OF HIS PLAN.

IT IS WITH DEEP DELIBERATION AND *CONCERN* THAT I TAKE THIS STEP --

-- FOR I'D HATE TO JEOPARDIZE RELATIONS WITH THE *SUPERHUMAN* COMMUNITY.

-- AND WE MUST INVESTIGATE ALL AVENUES. ACCORDINGLY, THE CITY WILL BEGIN TO *REGISTER* SUPERHUMANS --

-- IN ORDER TO GATHER INFORMATION TO HELP US *TRACK DOWN* THE KILLER. ALL INFORMATION WILL BE KEPT *CONFIDENTIAL*, AND --

MR. *MAYOR!* DO YOU PLAN TO REGISTER *ALL* THE HEROES?

FOR NOW, WE'LL ONLY BE REGISTERING THOSE WITH *MYSTIC POWERS.* IT'S *INFORMATION* WE'RE INTERESTED IN, NOT CONTROL.

AND WHAT IF THE HEROES WON'T *COOPERATE?*

BUT IT SEEMS OBVIOUS WE FACE AN *UNKNOWN* SUPERHUMAN HERE --

E.A.G.L.E. TROOPERS WILL ARRIVE *TOMORROW,* TO BEGIN THE REGISTRATION PROCESS. IT IS OUR *HOPE* --

-- THAT THE HEROES WILL AID OUR EFFORT BY POLICING *THEMSELVES.*

THE HALL *ERUPTED* WITH QUESTIONS. WHAT INFORMATION WOULD BE *SOUGHT?* WOULD THERE BE *SANCTIONS* FOR NON-COMPLIANCE?

E.A.G.L.E. -- THE *EXTRANORMAL ACTIVITIES GARRISON FOR LAW ENFORCEMENT* -- USUALLY CAME IN *AFTER* THE HEROES --

-- TAKING CUSTODY OF *VILLAINS,* GUARDING DAMAGED *PROPERTY,* ETC. TO BRING THEM IN ON SOMETHING LIKE THIS WAS *NEW.*

76

FOR A WHILE, IT FELT LIKE THE REGISTRATION ISSUE BECAME BIGGER THAN THE *KILLINGS*, THOUGH THEY NEVER FADED AWAY.

NONE OF THE CITY'S HEROES CAME *FORWARD* -- AND I DIDN'T KNOW WHAT TO THINK ANY MORE THAN THE *PEOPLE* DID.

SO WHAT DO *WE* DO?

DO? WE'RE STILL AFTER THE *GUNSLINGER*, AREN'T WE?

IT MAY NOT BE A *SEXY* CASE -- AND HIS VICTIMS AREN'T AS YOUNG OR AS INNOCENT AS MISS *FELTON* --

NO -- I MEAN ABOUT THE *REGISTRATION.*

DO WE -- ARE WE --

-- BUT THEY'RE STILL *LIVES,* AND THEY'RE STILL WORTH *PROTECTING.*

BRIAN. ARE YOU ASKING ME IF I HAVE *MYSTIC* POWERS?

I -- UH -- NO -- I JUST --

LET'S GO. THE NIGHT *AWAITS.*

-- UH --

IT TURNED OUT THAT THE MEN THE GUNSLINGER'D RECENTLY KILLED ALL SERVED IN THE SAME SQUAD IN *VIET NAM.*

WE WENT LOOKING FOR PEOPLE WHO MIGHT *KNOW* SOMETHING ABOUT THAT SQUAD, AND I LEARNED ANOTHER TRICK OF THE TRADE.

THE ONES WHO MOST WANT TO *AVOID* YOU --

-- *THOSE* ARE THE GUYS TO TALK TO.

TRENCH...

NO! I DON'T --

DEAD *END*, TRENCH.

CHARLIE COMPANY, TRENCH. YOU WEREN'T ONE OF THEM, BUT YOU KNEW THEM. *TELL ME.*

GEEZ, I DON'T -- I MEAN, SOME OF THOSE GUYS, THEY'RE *BAD NEWS!* I DON'T WANNA --

LOOK AT ME, TRENCH. I'M RIGHT *HERE* -- AND I'M NOT EXACTLY GOOD NEWS...

UH --

WELL, THESE IS JUST *RUMORS,* MIND YOU? STUFF I HEARD? WORD IS, GUYS IN CHARLIE WERE PART OF A MAJOR *HEROIN* RING --

-- EVEN FRAGGED THEIR *SARGE* WHEN HE WOULDN'T GO ALONG -- AND HIM WITH A PREGNANT GOOK *WIFE,* TOO...

A PREGNANT *WIFE.* WELL, WELL. IT LOOKS AS IF OUR QUARRY'S MOTIVATIONS MAY BE *PERSONAL,* FOR ONCE...

I HEARD THE NEWS, AND I GUESS I SHOULD'VE BEEN *GLAD.* BUT I KEPT HEARING HIS *VOICE* IN MY HEAD, LIKE OILED GRAVEL --

"ARE YOU ASKING ME IF I HAVE *MYSTIC POWERS?*"

BUT NOTHING MORE HAPPENED. WE KEPT LOOKING FOR *GUN-SLINGER,* THE SHADOW HILL KILLER ELUDED *EVERYONE* --

-- AND THE PEOPLE SHAKILY SUPPORTED THEIR *HEROES* --

-- OR AT LEAST, THEY DID UNTIL HONOR GUARD FOUGHT THE *FRIGIANS* AND THE *THERMIANS* IN ANTARCTICA.

I'LL NEVER *UNDERSTAND* IT. THE FRIGIANS AND THE THERMIANS HAD BEEN INTERMITTENTLY ATTACKING US OR EACH OTHER FOR *YEARS* --

-- SOMETHING ABOUT OUR WORLD BEING THE *INTERFACE* BETWEEN THEIRS, SO THEY HAD TO GO THROUGH US TO GET TO THE OTHER.

THEY WERE A *THREAT.* NO TWO WAYS ABOUT IT, THEY WERE A *GRAVE DANGER.*

BUT IT DIDN'T SEEM TO *MATTER* THAT IF HONOR GUARD HADN'T STOPPED THEM, THEY COULD HAVE *SHATTERED* THE PLANET.

ALL THAT SEEMED TO MATTER TO MOST OF *ASTRO CITY,* IT SEEMED --

-- WAS THAT HONOR GUARD WASN'T *HERE.*

-- GOT THREE *KIDS!* AND WHILE SAMARITAN'S DANCING AROUND WITH SOME *SNOWMEN,* THEY COULD --

-- THEY EVEN *CARE?* DON'T THEY REALIZE --

-- GOT TO WAIT IN *LINE* NOW? LET 'EM GO MESS WITH THOSE GUYS *AFTER* THEY CATCH THE --

-- NOT GOING TO *HELP,* THEY COULD AT LEAST COOPERATE WITH THE *MAYOR'S* --

-- *TYPICAL!* ALL THE TIME IN THE WORLD FOR COSMIC CRAP, BUT WHEN IT'S LITTLE GIRLS DYING --

SOMETHING SEEMED TO *CHANGE,* THEN.

IT WASN'T EVERYONE. FOR ALL THE PEOPLE WHO "GREETED" THE FIRST FAMILY ON THEIR RETURN FROM THE *MIRROR GALAXY* --

DO YOUR JOB!

WE WERE HERE FIRST

STOP THE KILLING

WHERE WERE YOU?

-- THERE WERE THOSE WHO FORMED A *HUMAN CHAIN* --

CATCH *KILLERS*, NOT *HEROES*!

REGISTRATION'S FOR *ZEROES*!

-- TO BLOCK *E.A.G.L.E.* TROOPERS FROM SEIZING THE *SUPERHUMAN STUDIES DEPARTMENT'S* RECORDS AT *FBU.*

BUT THE BAD STUFF WAS BAD ENOUGH... AND GETTING *WORSE.*

YOU WANT TO SAVE *SOULS*, YOU FREAKS?

SAVE *SARA-LYNNE FELTON'S!*

THEY -- THEY WERE CHEERING US -- ONLY *WEEKS* AGO!

HOW DID IT CHANGE -- SO *FAST*?

NOTHING'S CHANGED, BRIAN.

BOTH FACES ARE ALWAYS THERE. THE DARKER ONE STAYS SHADOWED, MOST OF THE TIME...

...BUT IT'S COME OUT INTO THE LIGHT OVER LESS THAN *THIS...!*

I THOUGHT IT WOULD *FADE AWAY.* I THOUGHT IT WOULD *HAVE* TO.

SOMEONE WOULD CATCH THE *KILLER,* AND EVERYTHING WOULD GO BACK TO *NORMAL.*

81

I WATCHED THE NEXT DAY, AS MORDECAI CHALK *ENTERED* SHADOW HILL, LOADED FOR BEAR, FULL OF ASSURANCES OF SPEEDY *SUCCESS.*

THE HILLERS ROLLED BACK THE BARRICADES TO LET HIM IN, AND THE CITY SIDE *CHEERED* LIKE THEY'D *BURST* FROM IT --

-- BUT THE STREETS OF SHADOW HILL STAYED *SILENT.* SO SILENT --

-- I COULDN'T HELP BUT *SHIVER.*

SO HE WENT IN. BIG *DEAL!* IT'S NOT LIKE HE'S DOING ANYTHING JACK-IN-THE-BOX OR *QUARREL* HASN'T DONE!

JUST BECAUSE HE *TALKS* BIG --

HE'S OFFERING PEOPLE *HOPE.* IT'S ONLY HUMAN NATURE TO *GRASP* AT IT.

WELL, I THINK IT *STINKS!* IF HE *SUCCEEDS* --

IF HE SUCCEEDS, THE THREAT WILL BE *GONE.* THAT'S WHAT *MATTERS* --

-- AND THAT'S *ALL* THAT MATTERS.

HUH--?! I HIT YOU! I HIT YOU *DEAD CENTER!*

OH?

MAYBE YOU'RE *SLIPPING,* GUNSLINGER. MAYBE YOUR *CONSCIENCE* IS BOTHERING YOU.

EITHER WAY --

KRNCH

-- YOUR *GUNS* AREN'T GOING TO DO YOU ANY *GOOD.*

? ?

THOSE WERE HAND-CRAFTED -- AND *SOLID STEEL!* LOOKS LIKE IT'S TIME TO *BUG OUT* --

SNEK

-- BUT I'LL BE *BACK,* PADRE, I'LL BE *BACK!*

NO. YOU'RE NOT GOING TO *ESCAPE.*

THIS ENDS *TONIGHT.*

HIS JET-BOOTS WERE OBVIOUSLY AN *EMERGENCY MEASURE.* THEY DIDN'T FLY THAT *SWIFTLY* --

-- AND IT DIDN'T LOOK LIKE THEY'D CARRY HIM THAT *FAR,* EITHER --

I'D ALMOST CAUGHT UP TO THEM WHEN THE GUNSLINGER'S *JETS* SPUTTERED OUT --

-- AND --

OUT OF MY WAY! I CAN *STILL* GET AWAY! I CAN LOSE MYSELF IN THESE --

NO, GUNSLINGER.

IT'S OVER.

AND THE *PEOPLE* --

-- THE *LOOK* ON THEIR FACES --

-- THEY WERE *SCARED* OF SOMETHING -- BACKING AWAY, CROSSING THEMSELVES. THEY WERE SCARED OF *SOMETHING* --

-- AND IT *WASN'T* THE GUNSLINGER --

AND IT *ECHOED* AGAIN. I TRIED TO TELL MYSELF THERE WAS NOTHING TO IT, THAT HE WAS JUST MAKING A *JOKE*. BUT STILL --

-- "ARE YOU ASKING ME IF I HAVE *MYSTIC POWERS?*"

WHAT'S GOING *ON?* WHY ARE THEY -- ?

I THOUGHT I TOLD YOU TO STAY *BACK.*

WELL, NO MATTER. WE'D BETTER GET HIM TO THE NEAREST *POLICE STATION.* THEY'LL BE HAPPY TO HAVE HIM IN *CUSTODY.*

AND THAT WAS THAT. ONLY IT *WASN'T.*

THERE WERE *FIRES* ON SHADOW HILL THAT NIGHT.

FIRES IN THE *DOORWAYS* -- THAT PRODUCED A STRANGE, PUNGENT SMOKE THAT WAFTED TOWARD US EVEN WITH NO *BREEZE.*

THE OTHER KIDS SAID THIS HAD HAPPENED *BEFORE,* THAT IT HAPPENED EVERY NOW AND THEN --

-- BUT RIGHT NOW, IT WAS JUST ONE MORE *THING* --

-- AND PEOPLE DIDN'T LIKE IT. THERE WAS MORE TALK OF *RAZING* THE HILL --

-- OF *DYNAMITING* THE MOUNTAIN AND BURYING THE WHOLE PLACE UNDER TONS OF *ROCK* --

-- AND THE NEXT DAY, THE MAYOR STATIONED *E.A.G.L.E.* TROOPS ALL ALONG THE BARRICADES.

NOBODY WAS DOING ANYTHING *CRAZY.* NOT ON *HIS* WATCH, HE SAID. AND MORE --

THIS ATMOSPHERE OF *FEAR,* OF *PARANOIA* -- OF NEIGHBOR SUSPECTING NEIGHBOR, AND PANIC IN THE *STREETS* --

-- I LAY IT AT THE DOORSTEP OF OUR SO-CALLED *HEROES,* AND THEIR PASSION FOR PRIVACY, FOR *SECRECY!*

WE HAVE GOTTEN USED TO *MASKS!* TO FACADES, TO STONEWALLING! WE'VE SOLD OUR SOULS FOR *SAFETY* -- AND *THIS* IS THE PRICE! I HEREBY SERVE NOTICE ON THEM *ALL* -- ON THEIR COSTUMES AND FORTRESSES AND THEIR DISDAIN FOR THE *LAW!*

-- IF I HAVE TO BRING EVERY SINGLE ONE OF THEM DOWN TO *DO* IT!

A FEW MONTHS *EARLIER,* THAT SPEECH WOULD HAVE GOTTEN HIM IMPEACHED.

I DON'T CARE WHAT THEY'RE HIDING -- WHO THEY'RE *PROTECTING!* I *WILL* MAKE THIS CITY SAFE AGAIN --

BUT NOW, IT GOT SCATTERED, NERVOUS *APPLAUSE.*

I COULDN'T *WORRY* ABOUT IT. I HAD *OTHER* THINGS ON MY MIND.

I SPENT THE DAY ON THE *BIRO ISLAND* FERRY, STARING AT THE WATER AS WE SHUTTLED BACK AND FORTH --

AND DESPITE THE HEAT -- ALL I COULD FEEL WAS *COLD.*

-- ENVELOPING MYSELF IN THE SILENCE OF FAMILIES HEADED TO VISIT *CONVICTS,* OF PEOPLE WITH *IRON BARS* IN THEIR THOUGHTS.

BIRO ISLAND FERRY

BRIAN...

YOU *CHALLENGED* ME! YOU *DARED* ME TO FIND OUT YOUR SECRETS! YOU *JOKED* ABOUT IT, DAMMIT!

YOU... ...YOU'RE A VAMPIRE, AREN'T YOU?

YOU SNUCK UP *BEHIND* ME WHEN I WAS LOOKING IN A *MIRROR!* YOU DON'T HAVE A *REFLECTION!*

WELL? *AREN'T* YOU?!

AH, YOUNG BRIAN. WELL... WELL *DONE.*

TO BE CONTINUED

ASTRO CITY DEPT. OF PUBLIC WORKS

CHAPTER 4

THE FIRST PLACE WAS ONE OF THE DEACON'S *DRUG DROPS* --

-- WHERE THE *STREET DEALERS* PICKED UP THEIR STOCK IN TRADE FROM THE LOCAL *SUPPLIERS.*

THAT'S WHERE I STARTED TO GET AN INKLING ABOUT WHAT HE WAS *DOING.*

THEN IT WAS UP THE CHAIN, TO THE *MONEY MEN* -- THE MEN WHO FUNNELED ALL THE *CASH* THAT CAME BACK IN TO THE DEACON.

THE *DEACON!*

TELL HIM! TELL HIM I'M *COMING* FOR HIM -- -- TELL HIM HIS *REIGN ENDS TONIGHT!*

WITHIN *MINUTES* AFTER THAT STRIKE, THE DEACON GOT HIS *SOLDIERS* OUT ON THE STREET --

-- ARMED TO THE TEETH AND *READY* FOR THE CONFESSOR.

I DON'T *FEAR* YOU. AND I *DON'T* WANT TO KILL YOU.

AS FOR HUNTING YOU DOWN --

STAY *BACK* -- !

I DON'T KNOW MUCH *ABOUT* YOU. BUT I KNOW YOU'RE A *GOOD MAN.* I'VE SEEN YOU SAVE *DOZENS* OF LIVES -- -- SEEN YOU CAPTURE *THIEVES,* TRACK DOWN *MURDERERS* --

ALL THIS, *TONIGHT* -- YOU DON'T HAVE *ANYTHING* TO PROVE.

BUT I --

AND YOU *WANTED* ME TO FIGURE THIS OUT. YOU *LET* ME. MAYBE I PUT THE *CLUES* TOGETHER, BUT YOU LET ME SEE THEM. YOU DIDN'T *HAVE* TO.

YOU'RE...

...YOU'RE MORE *OBSERVANT* THAN I'D THOUGHT.

I'D LIKE TO *UNDERSTAND.* IF YOU CAN *TELL* ME ABOUT IT.

YOU'VE *EARNED* IT. BUT IT'S ALMOST *DAWN,* AND I HAVE TO GO. WE'LL TALK *TONIGHT.*

AND FOR THE FIRST TIME --

-- I *SAW* HIM VANISH.

AND THEN I WAS *ALONE,* IN A SWIRL OF QUESTIONS. HOW DID HE... *BECOME* WHAT HE WAS? WHY DID HE *DO* WHAT HE DID?

WOULD HE EVEN *SHOW UP* WHEN THE SUN WENT DOWN AGAIN?

AND I LOOKED AT THE *SKY,* AND THE LIGHTNING HAD EASED OFF FOR A WHILE --

-- BUT THERE WERE *OTHER* LIGHTS IN THE SKY --

-- AND I COULDN'T HELP BUT *WONDER* --

IT WAS ALL OVER
THE *NEWS*, OF
COURSE --

-- SPOKESMEN FOR *HONOR GUARD* SAY THE SHIP APPEARS TO BE A *SCOUT SHIP*, AND OPENED FIRE WHEN THEY INVESTIGATED --

-- BUT THAT AT THIS POINT THEY DO NOT KNOW WHERE IT *CAME* FROM, OR WHETHER *OTHER* SHIPS ARE OUT THERE.

KAST 7
NEWSFLASH

THIS HAS TOUCHED OFF *ANOTHER* CONFRONTATION BETWEEN THE *MAYOR'S OFFICE* AND THE SUPERHEROES --

-- AS THE MAYOR DIRECTED HONOR GUARD TO TURN THE SHIP AND ITS OCCUPANTS OVER TO THE *FEDERAL GOVERNMENT* --

KBAC

" -- AND THE TEAM *DEMURRED* -- "

SURE, WE'LL TURN IT OVER, BUT WE'VE GOT TO FIND SOME *STUFF* OUT FIRST. WE'RE HOPING TO CONTACT *STARWOMAN* --

-- FIND OUT IF *HER* PEOPLE KNOW ANYTHING ABOUT THESE GUYS.

QUARREL *of* HONOR GUARD

" -- LEADING TO AN *ANGRY RESPONSE* FROM THE MAYOR -- "

HONOR GUARD -- AND ALL THE SO-CALLED *"HEROES"* -- HAVE TO LEARN THAT THIS PLANET IS *NOT* THEIR PRIVATE PLAYGROUND.

THEIR FLOUTING AUTHORITY LIKE THIS SHOWS CONTEMPT AND ARROGANCE -- AND IT WILL *NOT* BE TOLERATED!

IN *OTHER* NEWS, THERE IS STILL NO WORD FROM PROFESSIONAL MONSTER-HUNTER *MORDECAI CHALK* --

-- WHO ENTERED SHADOW HILL *DAYS* AGO IN SEARCH OF THE *SERIAL KILLER* PLAGUING AREA NEIGHBORHOODS.

CHALK HAD PROMISED TO MAKE *REGULAR* REPORTS, BUT HIS LAST CONTACT CAME *TUESDAY*, AND WAS DROWNED OUT BY *STATIC...*

"THE *RAPIER* CAME TO THE MUSEUM TO USE THE *CONTACT MATRIX* DISPLAYED THERE, TO CALL EX-GUARD-MEMBER *STARWOMAN* --

"-- BUT WAS *PREVENTED* FROM ENTERING BY E.A.G.L.E. TROOPS. THERE WAS NO VIOLENCE, BUT *WITNESSES* SAY --"

I DON'T *LIKE* THIS. THEY'RE SO *POWERFUL* -- AND IT SEEMS LIKE EVERY DAY THERE'S *MORE* OF 'EM.

IF WE CAN'T *CONTROL* THEM...

WHAT DO YOU MEAN, *CONTROL THEM?*

THEY'RE NOT DOING ANYTHING *WRONG!* IT'S THE *MAYOR* WHO'S --

YOU'RE *YOUNG.* YOU DON'T REMEMBER THE *SEVENTIES.*

HUH? WHAT DOES *THAT* --

IF YOU *REMEMBERED,* YOU WOULDN'T BE SO READY TO *PRAISE* -- SO TRUSTING OF ANYONE IN A *CAPE.*

DO SOME *READING. TALK* TO SOME PEOPLE. IT WAS A *BAD TIME,* BACK THEN --

-- AND IT MAY BE STARTING *AGAIN...*

I DIDN'T PUT ON MY *COSTUME* THAT DAY, AND NOT JUST BECAUSE IT WAS SO *HOT* OUT.

I JUST WANDERED AROUND. *LISTENING.*

LISTENING UNEASILY.

BUT I *DID* PUT IT ON WHEN NIGHT FELL. I PUT IT ON, AND WENT TO OUR -- TO *HIS* HEADQUARTERS.

Brian—
The
North
Tower
C...

"I SPENT MUCH *TIME* IN THE HILLS, VISITING THE INJURED, BRINGING THEM THE BLESSINGS OF *GOD* --

"-- AND AT THE HOME OF ONE STONEWORKER, WHO'D BROKEN HIS LEG --

"-- I SAW A YOUNG WOMAN I ASSUMED TO BE HIS *DAUGHTER.*

"I FOUND MORE *REASONS* TO VISIT, TELLING MYSELF HE WAS AN *INFLUENTIAL MAN* IN THE COMMUNITY --

"-- AND THAT HIS GOOD OPINION OF US WOULD *HELP* OUR EFFORTS.

"BUT I WAS LYING TO MYSELF, AND I KNEW IT. I WAS A *SINNER,* AND MY WEAKNESS BROUGHT ME BACK AGAIN AND AGAIN --

"-- HOPING TO CATCH ANOTHER GLIMPSE OF THOSE *FLASHING EYES.*

"I WAS A *SINNER,* AND I PAID THE *PRICE* --

"-- FOR LABORERS WERE NOT THE *ONLY* ONES WHO HAD COME OVER ON THE GREAT SHIPS THAT CROSSED THE *ATLANTIC.*

"THE VAMPIRE *DRAINED* ME, AND LEFT MY CORPSE BURIED IN GARBAGE AND *FILTH.* AND THREE DAYS LATER --"

"-- I AROSE."

Uh.

WELL, IF -- I MEAN I'M NOT DISPUTING YOU, I *BELIEVE* YOU, BUT IF -- YOU WEAR A *CROSS* ON YOUR CHEST. DOESN'T THAT -- WELL, *HURT?*

YES.

IT IS *MEANT* TO. IT IS A FORM OF *MORTIFICATION.*

IT IS *MORE* THAN THAT. THE PAIN IS A *FOCUS* -- IT REMINDS US OF OUR *FRAILTY,* AND DISTRACTS OUR MINDS FROM *SIN.*

YOU MEAN, LIKE MONKS *WHIPPING* THEMSELVES -- AS PUNISHMENT FOR, UM, *SINFUL THOUGHTS?*

NOBODY -- NOBODY REALLY *DOES* THAT, DO THEY?

I... *THIRST,* LIKE ALL VAMPIRES. BUT THE PAIN -- IT HELPS ME TO *RESIST,* GIVES ME SOMETHING ELSE TO FEEL IN ITS

AND IT WORKS? I MEAN, YOU... uh... ...YOU'VE NEVER *KILLED* ANYONE?

PLEASE... ...DO NOT *ASK* ME THAT...

SO, UM, *OKAY*...

YOU'RE A *VAMPIRE.* YOU'RE... *FIGHTING* THE CURSE. SO...

...WHY *THIS?*

WHY BE A *SUPER-HERO?*

I...TRIED TO *LIVE*, IF NOT AS A MAN, THEN STILL AS A *PRIEST*.

"I TRIED TO ATONE FOR MY SIN THROUGH *STUDY*, THROUGH *WRITING*...

"BUT WHEN I LEFT MY WRITING FOR OTHERS TO *FIND*, THEY TRIED TO HUNT ME DOWN, TO *KILL ME*.

"I ELUDED THEM, *HID* FROM THEM...

"...AND IN THE END, THEY GAVE UP THE *SEARCH*, AND WALLED OFF THE WING OF THE CATHEDRAL THEY THOUGHT WAS *MY LAIR*...

"...LEAVING IT *UNFINISHED, UNCONSECRATED,* EVEN *TODAY*.

"FOR YEARS, I DREW INTO *MYSELF*, AVOIDING ALL CONTACT... SUSTAINING MYSELF THROUGH *PRAYER*.

"BUT I FELT MYSELF... MY *HUMANITY*... SLIPPING FURTHER AND FURTHER AWAY. AND I GREW *FEARFUL* OF WHAT I MIGHT BECOME.

"BY THEN, HOWEVER, THE MASKED HERO CALLED *AIR ACE* HAD EMERGED...

"...HE, AND OTHERS *LIKE HIM*."

I DON'T *BUY* IT. IT'S *MORE* THAN THAT.

YOU WANTED SOMEONE YOU DIDN'T HAVE TO *LIE* TO.

AND... IF THAT'S *TRUE...*?

I HAVE TO GO. I HAVE TO *THINK.*

I'LL... I'LL SEE YOU *LATER,* OKAY?

I SLEPT *FITFULLY* FOR THE REST OF THE NIGHT, AND INTO THE *MORNING.*

AND BY THE NEXT *AFTERNOON* --

THAT NIGHT, I WORE MY *COSTUME.* IT WOULD HAVE FELT LIKE COWARDICE NOT TO. I AVOIDED SEVERAL *E.A.G.L.E. PATROLS* --

-- STOPPED A FEW *LOOTERS* WHO THOUGHT THE MAYOR'S ORDER MEANT THEY HAD A LICENSE TO *STEAL* --

-- AND ENDED UP AT THE *CATHEDRAL.* LOOKING OUT AT THE CITY, TRYING TO SEE WHAT THE *CONFESSOR* DID.

BUT ALL I SAW WERE *BUILDINGS.* BUILDINGS FULL OF UNGRATEFUL, SMALL-MINDED SHEEP WHO DIDN'T *DESERVE* THEIR HEROES --

THEY COULD HAVE *STOOD UP* TO HIM. THEY COULD HAVE TOLD HIM HE WAS *WRONG,* IF THEY DISAGREED...

YOU ARE *UNHAPPY* TONIGHT, YOUNG BRIAN.

I DON'T KNOW *HOW* I FEEL. EVERYTHING'S *SWIRLING AROUND,* AND I'M *CAUGHT UP* IN ALL OF IT, AND AT EVERY SIDE, EVERY *TURN* --

-- *NOTHING'S* WHAT IT LOOKS LIKE. NOTHING'S *EASY.* AND IT'S NOT LIKE I THOUGHT IT WAS GOING TO BE A *WALK IN THE PARK,* BUT --

THIS ISN'T WHAT I THOUGHT IT WOULD BE *LIKE.* IT ISN'T WHAT I THOUGHT AT *ALL.*

IT LOOKED SIMPLE... BUT IT'S *NOT.*

TO BE
CONTINUED

ASTRO CITY
DEPT. OF PUBLIC
WORKS

SIR!

IS HE -- ?

WHAT'S HIS --

WHAT *WAS* IT? WHAT DID HE *MEET* IN THERE?

I DON'T KNOW. BUT *WHATEVER* IT WAS, HE SURE AS HELL MET *SOMETHING.*

AND THERE YOU HAVE IT. HE MET... *SOMETHING.* AS TO THE *DETAILS* -- AT THIS POINT, ONLY *TIME* WILL TELL.

THE MAYOR ISSUED A *STATEMENT* THIS MORNING, UPON HEARING OF THE *TRAGIC DEVELOPMENTS...*

-- CALL ON ALL *ASTRO* CITIZENS TO *PULL TOGETHER* IN THIS CRISIS -- AND A CRISIS IS *INDEED* WHAT WE FACE.

CRIME IS *UP* -- *POLICE* AND *E.A.G.L.E. TROOPS* ARE STRETCHED TO THE LIMIT DEALING WITH THE SO-CALLED *SUPERHEROES* --

-- AND NOW *THIS.*

THE BOTTOM LINE IS THE *SAFETY* OF THE *CITIZENRY* --

-- BUT THE "HEROES" SEEM TO HAVE *FORGOTTEN* THAT. ONCE AGAIN, I URGE THEM -- *HELP US. WORK WITH US.* YOUR INTRANSIGENCE IS DIVISIVE --

-- AND ANYTHING LESS THAN FULL COOPERATION IS HARMFUL TO US ALL.

PSHYEAH, *RIGHT.* HE IS SO FULL OF IT.

HE'S A POLITICIAN, WHADDYA *EXPECT?* C'MON, GILLIGAN'S ISLAND'S ON.

THE MAYOR WAS *WRONG.* THE HEROES WERE DOING *FINE* -- OR AT LEAST DOING THEIR *BEST* --

-- UNTIL THE MAYOR DECIDED HE WANTED 'EM ALL UNDER HIS *THUMB*, AND DECLARED THEM *OUTLAWS* WHEN THEY WOULDN'T PLAY.

WE MUST WORK TOGETHER, IF WE --

K K K

-- BUT LOVEYYYY --!

AND LOOK WHAT HE *GOT*.

WINGED VICTORY WAS CAPTURED, WHEN *E.A.G.L.E. TROOPS* INVADED ONE OF HER SCHOOLS --

-- AND THEY *LOCKED HER UP*, JUST LIKE THEY'D DONE WITH MOST OF THE *IRREGULARS* ALREADY.

THE 'REGS THEY DIDN'T HAVE IN JAIL WERE ON THE *LAM*, UNABLE TO HELP.

THE *CROSSBREED* WERE GONE, TOO -- NOBODY'D SEEN THEM FOR DAYS --

-- AND EVEN *HONOR GUARD* HAD TAKEN TO THEIR AIRBORNE HEADQUARTERS, CUTTING OFF ALL *COMMUNICATION* --

-- AND STILL APPARENTLY INVESTIGATING THE *ALIEN SHIP* THEY'D CAPTURED.

THE AIR FORCE WERE SCOURING THEIR HQ'S *LAST-KNOWN* LOCATION -- BUT EVEN THEIR MOST *SOPHISTICATED SENSORS* CAME UP WITH NOTHING.

STILL, *SAMARITAN* HAD BEEN SIGHTED IN NEW DELHI, FIGHTING ALONGSIDE THE *UNCLEAN* --

-- AND OTHER REPORTS HAD HIM IN CANADA, JAPAN, AND THE CANARY ISLANDS. *HE* WASN'T QUITTING.

YES. BUT YOU'RE OBVIOUSLY *CONFLICTED* ABOUT SOMETHING...

LOOK AT THE *PATTERNS.* SEE WHAT DOESN'T *FIT.* THAT'S WHAT YOU *TOLD* ME.

SURELY YOUR FABULOUS DETECTIVE SKILLS CAN HANDLE *THIS.*

BRIAN, I...

WHAT?!

BUT WHATEVER IT WAS, HE DIDN'T SAY IT. HE JUST BOWED HIS HEAD FOR A MOMENT, THEN TURNED, AND...

NEVER MIND. I'M GOING OUT. YOU'RE FREE TO *JOIN* ME, IF YOU'D LIKE.

I'D BEEN DOING IT FOR DAYS. *ACCOMPANYING* HIM, BUT STRICTLY ON A DAY-TO-DAY BASIS.

I DIDN'T KNOW WHAT I WANTED TO *DO.*

-- BUT HE WAS A *VAMPIRE.* AND HE HADN'T *TOLD* ME.

IT DIDN'T *FEEL* RIGHT. *NOTHING* FELT RIGHT.

I COULDN'T *QUIT* -- NOT WHEN IT WOULD FEEL LIKE KNUCKLING UNDER TO THE *MAYOR.* BUT --

ALIEN *SHAPE-CHANGERS.*

VAMPIRES WHO *PRAYED* TO KEEP FROM DRINKING BLOOD.

MYSTERY KILLERS WHO COULDN'T BE *CAUGHT.*

THE *MAYOR.*

AND EVEN *HE* WASN'T *ALONE* -- THIS WASN'T THE ONLY CITY HAVING *HERO TROUBLE.*

IT WAS SUPPOSED TO MAKE *SENSE.* IT WAS SUPPOSED TO FIT *TOGETHER* SOMEHOW. BUT --

DOWN BELOW. LOOTERS.

GAUTRAY ELECTRONICS

LET ME *GUESS.* YOU THOUGHT THE *POLICE* WOULD BE BUSY CHASING THE CRIME-FIGHTERS --

-- AND THE *CRIMEFIGHTERS* WOULD BE BUSY BEING CHASED. *YES?*

H-*HUH?!* THE *CONFESSOR?*

I -- I THOUGHT THEY *OUTLAWED* YOU GUYS!

THEY *DID.*

YEAH, WELL -- MAYBE WE GONNA MAKE US A *CITIZEN'S ARREST,* HUH?

SNEK

CHK

BUT THEY OUTLAWED YOU *FIRST.*

SOUND BAFFLES TO MASK PULSE AND RESPIRATION. COOLANT SYSTEMS TO CUT DOWN ON *PERSPIRATION.*

MY COMPLIMENTS.

REMEMBER MEN, STUN CHARGES *ONLY* -- AT LEAST FOR *NOW.* WE BRING THESE TWO IN *ALIVE* IF WE CAN.

NOW, CONFESSOR. PUT YOUR HANDS --

-- HUH? WHERE'D HE -- ?

TAKE 'EM! TAKE 'EM!

I WAS ABLE TO ACCOUNT FOR *TWO* OF THEM --

uhhh...

STUN CHARGES, HUH?

GOOD.

-- BUT IN THE TIME *THAT* TOOK --

AND THAT'S *THAT*.

YOU -- YOU -- SO *FAST* -- -- WHAT IN GOD'S NAME *ARE* YOU?

WHAT *ARE* WE? WELL, SPEAKING ONLY FOR *MYSELF*, MIND YOU --

-- I'M A *TEENAGE BOY.* BRING *THAT* UP AT YOUR NEXT *STORMTROOPER STRATEGY SESSION.*

ENOUGH *GLOATING,* ALTAR BOY. IT'S TIME WE WERE AWAY.

GLOATING? ME?

THEY *DID* GET CRACKERJACK, THOUGH, THE NEXT DAY -- EVEN IF THEY WEREN'T ABLE TO DETERMINE HIS *REAL IDENTITY.*

AND *WORSE* --

-- E.A.G.L.E. SHIPS HAVE REPORTEDLY LOCATED AND CORDONED OFF HONOR GUARD'S *AIRBORNE HEAD-QUARTERS* --

-- AND EVEN THE *EXPERIMENTALS'* STASIS PODS HAVE BEEN *CONFISCATED.*

IF YOU QUIT, HE *WINS.*

SO WHAT?!

IT'S NOT LIKE ANYONE *CARES,* RIGHT? HECK, THEY'RE PRACTICALLY *CHEERING* HIM *ON!*

YOU'VE SEEN IT -- THEY THREW *GARBAGE* AT US!

AND IS *THAT* WHY WE DO WHAT WE DO? FOR *PUBLIC APPROVAL,* FOR *FAME?*

DO WE HELP PEOPLE BECAUSE THEY WILL BE APPROPRIATELY *GRATEFUL* -- OR MERELY BECAUSE THEY *NEED* THE HELP?

HE SOUNDED LIKE MY *DAD.*

IT'S NOT -- IT'S NOT THAT *SIMPLE* --

WHY *NOT?*

BECAUSE EVERYTHING'S *CHANGED.* BECAUSE THEY'RE TRYING TO LOCK US UP, OR *KILL* US! THAT MAKES THINGS *DIFFERENT!*

DOES IT? THINGS ALWAYS CHANGE, YOUNG BRIAN. THERE IS EBB AND FLOW, AS SOME VOICES GROW *LOUDER,* AND OTHERS *FADE.*

BUT UNDERNEATH, THE WORLD IS STILL THE *SAME,* STILL A SHADOWED PATHWAY THROUGH FIELDS OF *GOOD* AND FORESTS OF *EVIL* --

-- WITH THE BATTERED, CONFUSED, OVERWHELMED SOULS WHO WALK IT CHOOSING *ANEW* EVERY DAY THAT THEY *LIVE.*

AND IF THE FORCES OF ANGER AND UNREASON ARE *GROWING*, IF HUMANITY IS LOSING SIGHT OF THEIR *PATH* --

-- THEN IS IT NOT ALL THE *MORE* CRUCIAL THAT THEY BE SHOWN THEIR *CHOICE*? THAT THEY BE SHOWN THE *WAY*?

I TAKE IT *BACK.* YOU'RE *WORSE* THAN MY DAD.

YOUR FATHER SOUNDS LIKE A VERY *ADMIRABLE* MAN. I'D LIKE TO HAVE *MET* HIM.

MY FATHER WAS AN *IDIOT* -- WHO DIED BROKE AND *LAUGHED AT!* AND YOU, A *VAMPIRE*, TALKING ABOUT THIS KIND OF --

-- DO YOU THINK FOR A *MINUTE* THAT ANYONE WOULD LISTEN TO YOU IF -- IF --

THEY *KNOW*, CONFESSOR! THEY *KNOW!*

ONE OF THE MAYOR'S STOOGES TOLD ME YESTERDAY, YOU SHOULD *LEAVE TOWN*, OR *RETIRE* --

-- *OR* THEY'D EXPOSE YOU! THEY'D LET PEOPLE KNOW WHAT YOU REALLY *ARE!*

THINK ABOUT HOW THEY'D *REACT* -- AND THEN ASK YOURSELF IF YOU STILL *WANT* TO SAVE 'EM ALL!

THEY...

...THEY *KNOW?*

BUT IF... IF THEY KNOW, ...IF ALL THEY WANT AND THEY'RE NOT IS FOR ME TO GET USING IT... OUT OF THEIR *WAY*... THEN...

THIS MEETING -- THESE *TROOPS!* WHEN DOES IT *START?*

IT'S PROBABLY *ALREADY* STARTING, BUT --

I'VE GOT TO GO. YOU STAY *HERE.*

BUT -- BUT --

-- IT'S NOT *FULL DARK* YET!

IT DIDN'T *STOP* HIM.

I'D BEEN *ANGRY,* AND WANTED TO HURT HIM. I'D *BELITTLED* HIM, TOLD HIM THE *DANGER* HE WAS IN -- AND IT DIDN'T SLOW HIM DOWN.

ALL HE SAW WAS SOME SORT OF DANGER TO *OTHERS* -- PATTERNS, AND SOMETHING THAT DIDN'T *FIT* --

-- AND ALL I COULD FEEL -- ALL I COULD FEEL --

-- WAS *SHAME.*

THE SAFETY OF THESE PEOPLE IS YOUR *LAST* CONCERN, IN THIS WORLD OR *ANY OTHER!* ISN'T IT?

ISN'T IT?!

GUARDS! *PROTECT* ME!

YES. *PROTECT* HIM. OR AT THE VERY LEAST...

...*TRY.*

I GOT THERE JUST AS THE *FIGHT* STARTED. HIM ALONE, AGAINST A *DOZEN* E.A.G.L.E. TROOPERS --

-- WITH WORSE COMING OFF THE SHIPS EVERY *MINUTE.*

HE PLOWED INTO THEM WITH *TOTAL ABANDON,* LIKE HE JUST DIDN'T CARE ABOUT HIS OWN *SAFETY* ANY MORE.

CHOOM

KRAK

CHOOM

AND HE HAD TO KNOW WHAT HE WAS *DOING.* HE *HAD* TO. LEAPING IN FRONT OF ALL THOSE *TELEVISION CAMERAS* --

136

AND THEN I COULDN'T *HOLD BACK* ANY LONGER. WHAT HE WAS JUST WASN'T IMPORTANT -- NOT NEXT TO *WHO* HE WAS.

NO! HOLD *ON,* CONFESSOR! HOLD ON -- *I'M ON MY WAY!*

I'D TOLD HIM THAT *BEFORE,* BUT UNTIL THEN, UNTIL I *SAW* HIM LIKE THAT, STILL STRUGGLING TO SAVE THE CITY --

-- I DON'T THINK I BELIEVED IT *MYSELF.*

RESTRAIN HIM!

BUT I WAS HIS *PARTNER.* I COULDN'T FAIL HIM ANY *FURTHER* -- EVEN IF PEOPLE *KNEW* --

WHAT? HE'S USING HIS POWERS! BREAKING *FREE!*

BUT -- THOSE CABLES ARE INFUSED WITH *HOLY WATER!* THEY SHOULD HOLD ANY --

-- EVEN IF THEY WERE ALREADY STARTING TO SAY THE *WORD* --

-- VAMPIRE --

-- HE'S --

-- VAMPIRE --

SO... MY SECRET IS *OUT.* BUT...

...BUT THERE ARE *WORSE* SECRETS TO BE REVEALED TONIGHT...

-- BUT I KNEW HE HAD A *WAY OUT* -- HAD SOME *PLAN* --

NOT BY *YOU,* MONSTER!

POOM

CHUKK

H-*UHH!*

He *HAD* TO. HE HAD TO HAVE A *PLAN.*

CONFESSOR!

NO NEED TO *PANIC,* ASTRO CITIZENS! *THIS* IS WHY WE'VE BROUGHT IN *EXTRA TROOPS* -- TO PROTECT YOU FROM THE SO-CALLED *"HEROES"* --

-- *"HEROES"* WHO'VE BEEN *PREYING* ON YOU!

AND ONCE WE THE TROOPS ARE *FULLY LANDED,* WE'LL *GUARANTEE* YOUR FUTURE SAFETY --

CHAPTER

MY FATHER'S SON

THE WORLD WAS AT WAR.

IN SYDNEY, THE *COLONIAL* AND *BULLROARER* STAVED OFF A *SQUADRON* OF ATTACK CRAFT --

-- WHILE *KOOKABURRA* AND *BARRIER* RALLIED THE OTHER AUSTRALIAN HEROES IN *CANBERRA*.

IN BOSTON, THE *SILVERSMITH* PROTECTED GOVERNMENT CENTER --

IN NEW YORK, *SKYSCRAPER* SOARED TO THE DEFENSE OF MANHATTAN --

IN ATLANTA, THE *REAL THING* LOOMED OVER THE CITY, SWATTING *GUNSHIPS* OUT OF THE SKY --

IN CHICAGO, IT WAS THE *UNTOUCHABLE* --

THE *HANGED MAN* WALLED OFF SHADOW HILL.

THE *FIRST FAMILY* SIDE-STEPPED THROUGH *DIMENSIONS* TO FREE THEMSELVES --

-- THEN BEGAN ANALYZING *CAPTURED ARMAMENTS,* HOPING TO FIND A WAY TO DESTROY THE ENEMIES' WEAPONS FROM A *DISTANCE.*

EVERYONE -- *NIGHTINGALE, SUNBIRD,* THE *OTHERS* -- DID THEIR PART.

AND AS FOR *ME* --

YOU'LL BE SAFE *HERE* FOR THE MOMENT. NOW, *EXCUSE* ME --

-- BUT I'M NEEDED *ELSEWHERE!*

BEHIND YOU, NOAH!

MY *THANKS,* MARY --

-- BUT I WAS CONFIDENT YOU'D BE ABLE TO *DEAL* WITH HIM.

NOW, JOSHUA -- HERD THEM TOWARD THEIR *SHIPS!* WE WANT THEM TO SEEK *COVER,* BUT NOT TO DEPART!

AND DANIEL -- NO *KILLING!*

WHAT?! BUT --

NO KILLING, DANIEL. *EVER.*

I COULDN'T *BELIEVE* IT.

NO ONE HAD SEEN THE *CROSSBREED* FOR *DAYS* -- AND EVERYONE ASSUMED THEY'D BEEN *HOUNDED OUT* OF THE CITY.

BUT HERE THEY WERE. *FIGHTING* -- RISKING THEIR *LIVES* --

I HAD TO *HELP* -- HAD TO PITCH IN --

KRAK

KZZAT

-- BUT --

AIHH!

YOU'RE STILL IN *SHOCK,* MY SON. YOU ARE IN NO SHAPE TO DO BATTLE. JUST *REST* -- LET *US* TAKE CARE OF THIS.

WE ARE SIMPLY GIVING THE *POPULACE* -- AND THE *HUMAN* TROOPS -- TIME TO GET OUT OF THE PARK, IN ANY CASE. ONCE *THAT'S* DONE --

ALL THE SHIPS *SECURED,* PETER?

THEY'RE NOT GOING *ANYWHERE!*

KRAK

KRAKK

KRKK

GOOD. A FEW THUNDERBOLTS TO SEAL THE *HATCHWAYS* --

"-- AND WE CAN *DEPART!*"

AND WE *DID.*

PETER'S ROCK-SHAPING POWERS CUT THROUGH THE *BEDROCK* BELOW THE CITY LIKE IT WAS *NOTHING* --

-- CARRYING US *AWAY* FROM THE PARK, AWAY FROM THE *THREAT.*

I SHOULD HAVE FELT *SAFE.*

INSTEAD, ALL I COULD THINK OF WAS THE *DARK* AND THE *COLD* -- AND MILLIONS OF TONS OF *ROCK,* PRESSING IN ON US --

ALL I COULD *THINK* OF --

-- WAS THE *CONFESSOR.*

I'D *SEEN* HIM -- SEEN HIS SKIN *BURN,* HIS FLESH *SHRIVEL AWAY* --

AND HE KNEW -- HE *KNEW* IT WOULD HAPPEN --

AND HE DIDN'T EVEN *HESITATE* --

ALTAR BOY? YOU'RE *SHAKING!*

HE HAS BEEN THROUGH A *GREAT DEAL,* MARY. HE NEEDS WARMTH, NEEDS HIS *WOUND* ATTENDED TO. FORTUNATELY --

153

IN THE END, OF COURSE, WE *WON*.

DR. *FURST* AND THE *FIRST FAMILY* MANAGED TO INTERCEPT THE *ENELSIANS'* COMMUNICATIONS --

-- AND ONCE THEY'D LOCATED THE *MOTHERSHIP* --

-- *SAMARITAN*, *WINGED VICTORY*, AND THE *GENTLEMAN* CAPTURED IT --

-- AND FORCED THE *SUPREME COMMANDRIX* TO ORDER A *RETREAT*.

THEY WOULDN'T BE *COMING BACK*, EITHER.

THERE WAS SOMETHING ABOUT A *GALACTIC COUNCIL*, AND *STARWOMAN'S* PEOPLE --

MOSTLY WHAT *WE* CARED ABOUT, THOUGH, WAS THAT THEY WERE *GONE*.

-- I NEVER GOT THE *DETAILS* STRAIGHT. BUT WHATEVER IT WAS, THE ENELSIANS WERE IN A LOT OF *TROUBLE*.

SAMARITAN HAD FOUND THE REAL *MAYOR STEVENSON,* TOO, IMPRISONED ON THE *MOTHERSHIP* --

-- ALONG WITH GOVERNMENT OFFICIALS FROM 45 *OTHER* CITIES AND COUNTRIES WORLDWIDE.

OFFICE of the MAYOR of

THANK YOU, *THANK* YOU. IT'S GOOD TO BE... *HERE.*

I'D LIKE TO *THANK* THE HEROES OF ASTRO CITY -- OF THE *WORLD* -- FOR THEIR UNWAVERING *FAITH,* EVEN DURING THIS ORDEAL.

AND I'D LIKE TO *APOLOGIZE* TO THEM --

-- FOR WHAT THEY'VE *SUFFERED* IN MY NAME.

THE MAYOR WENT ON, TO PRAISE THE SWIFT REACTION OF E.A.G.L.E., NATIONAL GUARD AND *ARMY* UNITS, BACKING UP THE HEROES --

-- AND TO PROMISE *SWIFT REPAIR* OF THE DAMAGE TO THE CITY.

AND THEN THE NEWSCAST WENT ON, TOO --

NEIGHBORHOOD WATCH GROUPS IN THE SHADOW HILL AREA ARE STANDING DOWN, AS WELL --

-- APPARENTLY SATISFIED THAT WITH THE DEATH OF THE CONFESSOR --

$1599⁹⁹

-- THE THREAT OF THE SHADOW HILL KILLER IS ENDED.

AUTHORITIES ARE BAFFLED AS TO WHY HE ATTACKED THE FALSE MAYOR STEVENSON, INDIRECTLY EXPOSING THE ALIENS --

ARC

WIDE SCREENS

-- BUT DEBATES BETWEEN F.B.U.'S SUPERHUMAN STUDIES AND THEOLOGICAL DEPARTMENTS HAVE BEEN SPIRITED --

-- AND A DEFINITIVE ANSWER IS EXPECTED WITHIN A WEEK.

26" Digital

$1599⁹⁹

Prices

Hey! HDTV is HERE!

Low Prices!

THEY'D NEVER FIGURE IT OUT. I *KNEW* THAT.

THEY WERE MAKING TOO MANY *ASSUMPTIONS*, FITTING THINGS INTO EASY *PATTERNS* --

-- WHICH IS WHAT THE ENELSIANS HAD *COUNTED* ON ALL ALONG.

THEY SNUCK IN THEIR *FIRST* AGENT WHILE HONOR GUARD'S *ALIEN DETECTOR* WAS MALFUNCTIONING --

-- AND OTHERS WHILE IT WAS *BUSY*, DETECTING THE *FRIGIANS*, THE *THERMIANS*, AND *OTHER* THREATS.

ALIENS DEFEATED!

THEY *DISCREDITED* THE HEROES RATHER THAN KILLING THEM AND RISKING *DISCOVERY* --

-- AND THEY WANTED THEM *ALIVE*, ANYWAY, TO SERVE AS *SLAVES.*

THEY HAD HONOR GUARD HEADQUARTERS CORDONED OFF TO JAM THE DETECTOR *ONCE AGAIN* --

-- THEN LANDED TROOPS IN *FORCE*, IN DISGUISE. THEY DIDN'T WANT A BATTLE TO BREAK OUT UNTIL THEY WERE IN *PLACE* --

-- UNTIL THEY HAD THE PLANET'S *INNOCENTS* HOSTAGE.

ONCE THEY'D FORCED A *SURRENDER*, THEY COULD ENSLAVE EARTH -- AND *FACE DOWN* THE GALACTIC COUNCIL.

NOW, THE AUTHORITIES WERE MAKING PLANS FOR *BACKUP* ALIEN DETECTORS --

-- AND STARWOMAN'S *CONTACT MATRIX* HAD BEEN RETURNED TO HONOR GUARD. THE SAME PLAN WOULDN'T WORK *AGAIN.*

BUT IT *ALMOST* WORKED. IT *COULD* HAVE WORKED.

AND SLOWLY, *TENTATIVELY*, THE CITY STARTED TO *HEAL*. YOU COULD *FEEL* IT.

AND I *NOTICED* SOMETHING.

THE PEOPLE WHO WERE *TALKING* THESE DAYS -- THE PEOPLE *PRAISING* THE HEROES, SHOWING *FAITH* IN THEM --

-- I DIDN'T THINK THEY WERE THE SAME PEOPLE AS *BEFORE*, WHO WERE SHOUTING FOR THE HEROES' *HEADS*.

BOTH FACES ARE ALWAYS THERE. THE DARKER ONE STAYS SHADOWED, MOST OF THE TIME...

...BUT IT'S COME OUT INTO THE LIGHT OVER LESS THAN *THIS...!*

AND I REMEMBERED SOMETHING THE *CONFESSOR* SAID --

AND I HAD A LOT TO *THINK* ABOUT -- ABOUT *MOBS*, AND HOW MUCH THEY SPEAK FOR *EVERYONE* --

-- AND ABOUT MY *DAD*, AND THE WAY HE VALUED *SICK KIDS* OVER DEADBEAT *PARENTS* --

BUT STILL, THERE WAS SOMETHING IN THE *AIR* -- SOMETHING THAT WASN'T DONE, SOMETHING STILL HOLDING ITS *BREATH* --

AND THEN ONE DAY, ANOTHER *BODY* TURNED UP, ON THE OUTSKIRTS OF SHADOW HILL --

-- ANOTHER BODY, *MUTILATED* LIKE THE OTHERS --

-- AND ALL OF A SUDDEN, EVEN THE *AIR* SMELLED DIFFERENT. *CLEANER.*

IT WAS ALMOST FUNNY, IN A *MACABRE* SORT OF WAY. PATTERNS EVERYWHERE, AND NOBODY *THOUGHT* --

-- NOBODY REALIZED THAT NOT *EVERYTHING* FITS TOGETHER.

THE ENELSIANS TOOK ADVANTAGE OF THE SHADOW HILL KILLER'S *EXISTENCE* -- AS THEY DID WITH TROUBLE IN OTHER CITIES --

-- BUT THAT WAS ALL. THERE WAS NO *CONNECTION.*

FUNNY HOW LIFE *WORKS,* SOMETIMES.

BUT THAT WAS IT, THAT WAS THE *END.* THE CITY SEEMED TO *EXHALE,* AFTER THAT.

AND THE MAYOR HELD A *MEMORIAL SERVICE* FOR THE DEAD, ONE COOL SUMMER EVENING IN *DEDICATION PARK* --

-- FOR THOSE WITH *RELATIVES* IN THE CITY, AND FOR THE OTHERS, THE *DRIFTERS* --

AND AFTER THE EULOGY WAS *OVER* --

HE DRIFTED ALONG THE LINE OF *RELATIVES,* LOOKING INTO THEIR EYES, ONE BY ONE.

AND HE DIDN'T SAY *ANYTHING* -- NOT ANYTHING ANY OF US COULD *HEAR,* ANYWAY --

-- BUT YOU COULD SEE THEM *RELAX.* YOU COULD SEE THAT THEY *KNEW* SOMETHING.

THAT SOMEHOW, HE'D LET THEM KNOW THAT *JUSTICE* HAD BEEN DONE.

HE HADN'T COME FOR *THANKS*, OR FOR PRAISE. HE'D COME TO GIVE *COMFORT*.

TO *HELP*.

AND IT WORKED. FOR EVERYONE BUT *ME*.

I WAS STILL ALL *TANGLED UP* INSIDE. THE CONFESSOR WAS *DEAD*. SNUFFED OUT -- JUST LIKE THAT. AND NOBODY *CARED*.

HE'D *SACRIFICED* HIMSELF -- KNOWINGLY AND *WILLINGLY* -- TO SAVE THE WORLD. AND NOBODY *KNEW*.

BUT FOR ALL I WANTED TO *SCREAM* AT EVERYONE -- TO SHAKE THEM UNTIL THEY *UNDERSTOOD* --

-- I KNEW HE WOULDN'T HAVE *MINDED*. IT WOULDN'T HAVE BOTHERED HIM. IT WAS THE *DOING* THAT WAS IMPORTANT --

-- NOT PEOPLE *KNOWING* WHAT HE'D DONE.

I HAD TO FIND MY ENDING *SOMEWHERE ELSE*.

AND A FEW DAYS LATER, I *REALIZED* --

-- I REALIZED *WHERE* I HAD TO GO.

BACK TO WHERE IT ALL *STARTED*.

Thomas William Kinney
1931 - 1982

Margaret Isles Kinney
1954 - 1982

LANGLANGLANGLANGLANGLANGLANGLAN

C'MON! MOVE YOUR *WORTHLESS* BUTTS! GET THESE FURS IN THE *TRUCK*, AND LET'S GET *OUTTA* HERE!

WE'RE GOIN', WE'RE GOIN'! JEEZ, THE COPS WON'T GET HERE FOR LIKE *FIVE* MINUTES!

YEAH, BUT --

THEY WERE *NERVOUS.* THEY'D HEARD *STORIES,* RUMORS.

WHISPERS OF SOMETHING THAT *COULDN'T* BE TRUE.

IT TOOK ME *FOUR YEARS. FOUR YEARS* OF TRAVEL. OF STUDY. *FOUR YEARS* OF *TRAINING.*

HE'S NOT *BACK.* HE *CAN'T* BE BACK. IT'S NOT *POSSIBLE.*

IT'S *NOT!*

WHO ARE YOU TRYING TO *CONVINCE,* GARRITY? THEM --

-- OR *YOURSELF?*

AND THE *VOICE MODULATOR* WORKED PERFECTLY.

WHO -- ?!

WH- *WHAT?*

OH MY *GOD!* OH MY *GOD!* OH MY *GOD!*

THEY WERE *NERVOUS.* THEY'D HEARD THE *RUMORS.* AND THEY CAME *PREPARED.*

HOLY WATER. GARLIC. CRUCIFIXES.

THE NEARNESS OF YOU

MIKE! EARTH TO MIKE! HAVE YOU HEARD A WORD I'VE SAID, MIKE? YOU LOOK AWFUL!

YOU'VE GOT TO GET SOME SLEEP, MAN...

THESE NEED TO BE TOTALLY REDONE, TENICEK. DID YOU EVEN BRING YOUR HEAD IN TO WORK THAT DAY?

I DON'T KNOW IF YOU'RE LOOKING FOR A NEW JOB, BUT LET ME TELL YOU --

-- YOU'RE THIS CLOSE TO NEEDING ONE. YOU GET ME?

I DON'T KNOW WHY I BOTHERED. EVERYONE SAYS YOU'RE A FLAKE, BUT YOU SEEMED LIKE A NICE GUY.

A WORD OF ADVICE, THE NEXT TIME YOU ASK SOMEONE TO DINNER? SHOW UP.

IT USED TO BE KIND OF NICE, WHEN IT ONLY HAPPENED ONCE EVERY COUPLE OF MONTHS OR SO.

A MYSTERY GIRL. HIS "DREAM GIRL," HE CALLED HER TO HIMSELF. BUT THAT WAS BEFORE IT WAS ONCE A WEEK. THEN TWICE. THEN --

AND IT'S NOT EVEN LIKE SHE'S HIS TYPE -- OR WHAT HE ALWAYS THOUGHT WAS HIS TYPE.

SHE'S NOT THE KIND OF WOMAN WHO TURNS HIS HEAD ON THE STREET. NOT WHAT HE'D PICK, IF YOU ASKED HIM.

BUT STILL -- HE GOES TO **SLEEP** --

-- AND HE'S SEEN THAT SMILE A **MILLION** TIMES. HE KNOWS JUST HOW SHE LIKES TO HAVE HER **NECK** RUBBED.

HE KNOWS SO MUCH **ABOUT** HER --

-- AND IT'S **TERRIFYING.**

IS HE **CRACKING UP?** IS HE GOING **INSANE?** FOR GOD'S SAKE, WHAT COMES **NEXT?**

HE KNOWS HE'S NEVER MET HER. HE **KNOWS.**

MOM? HI. NO, I'M GOOD, I'M **FINE.**

LISTEN, MOM --

-- DO YOU REMEMBER A GIRL NAMED **MIRANDA?**

MAYBE A COUPLE OF YEARS **YOUNGER** THAN ME? SHORT DARK HAIR? REALLY LIGHT FRECKLES ACROSS THE BRIDGE OF HER **NOSE?**

BUT -- ALL THIS WAS SO LONG AGO --

-- WHAT DOES IT HAVE TO DO WITH ME -- ?

OKAY, OKAY, I GET THE MESSAGE.

I'LL WAIT AND SEE...

AND THE MISTS RISE UP AROUND HIM ONCE MORE --

-- AND THE TIME-KEEPER HAS ESCAPED FROM JAIL, BUT FINDS HIS PLANS BLOCKED ON ALL SIDES --

THE ALL-AMERICAN! THE LAMPLIGHTER! THE ASTRONAUT!

-- BLACKOUT BANDITS FOILED TODAY BY THE ALL-AMERICAN AND SLUGGER --

IS THERE NO END TO THESE COSTUMED CRUSADERS?!

VERY WELL! I'VE SPENT MY LIFE MASTERING TIME -- WORKING, WHILE OTHERS MOCKED ME AS AN IDIOTIC DREAMER!

IF THESE "SUPERHEROES" STAND IN MY WAY, I DEVISE A MEANS TO GO BACK IN TIME --

-- AND PREVENT THEM FROM EVER BEING BORN!

LIFE

Super Heroes in The South Pacific

Who Is the Lamplighter?

-- AND
WORSE --

ASTRO
CITY --

-- IT'S
DISAPPEAR-
ING!

-- AND HE SEES THE
LAST, DESPERATE
BATTLE -- THE
VICTORIOUS BATTLE --

-- TO REWEAVE
TIME -- TO UNDO
THE DAMAGE --

-- AND TO SET
ALL, ONCE MORE,
TO RIGHTS.

WHEN... WHEN DID THIS ALL HAPPEN?

YESTERDAY. FIVE DECADES AGO. DOES IT MATTER?

I... UNDERSTAND, I THINK.

SHE DIED, DIDN'T SHE? I KNEW HER, AND SHE DIED IN THAT...THAT MAELSTROM...

SHE WAS YOUR WIFE. AND SHE NEVER EXISTED.

THE CHRONAL RECONSTRUCTION WAS NOT EXACT.

MY... WIFE?

AIR ACE FIRST BATTLED THE BARNSTORMERS ON A SUNDAY, NOT A MONDAY... AND AS A RESULT, HER GRANDPARENTS NEVER MET.

FOR THE MOST PART, THE NEW REALITY IS A WHOLE. BUT CLOSE BONDS SUCH AS YOURS... THEY CREATE A WEAKNESS IN THE FABRIC OF TIME...

...ONE THAT COULD LET THROUGH... DANGEROUS THINGS. BUT THE WEAKNESS IS HEALED BY YOUR UNDERSTANDING.

I CANNOT RETURN HER TO YOU... THAT IS BEYOND EVEN MY POWER. BUT IF THE PAIN IS TOO MUCH...

... I CAN ALLOW YOU TO FORGET...

FORGET HER?

I... UH...

NO. I DON'T WANT TO FORGET.

AS YOU WISH.

YOU WILL NOT REMEMBER THIS VISIT, THOUGH YOUR SENSE OF UNDERSTANDING WILL REMAIN.

AND NOW, I HAVE OTHERS TO VISIT TONIGHT, SO...

WAIT!

OTHERS? WHAT -- UH -- WHAT DO MOST PEOPLE CHOOSE? DO THEY FORGET, OR --

FOR A MOMENT, HE THINKS HE SEES THE TWITCH OF A SMILE UNDER THAT BURLAP HOOD --

NO ONE FORGETS. NO ONE.

GOOD NIGHT, MICHAEL TENICEK. SLEEP WELL.

AND THEN HE'S GONE --

-- AND THE MEMORY OF HIM FADES LIKE SMOKE ON THE SUMMER BREEZE --

DRAMATIS PERSOI

STAR BRAND

MONK HOOD

COLLAR SY(

CLERICAL LOOK

EVENING STAR IT'S SYMBOL

PENTAGRAM

A BALD HEAD?

WHITE HEADRESS?

DARK PURPLE & WHITE TRIM

MAYBE EYES JUST TURN WHITE WHEN HE'S IN COSTUME

GLOWING EYES

The most compelling personality, set of superpowers, mission — none of it will matter if the character doesn't look right, if the idea at the character's core doesn't come through. And that can take a lot of work.

The Confessor was originally called "Vesper," which combined nighttime and a religious touch, but an independent comic called Vespers was announced, so we renamed him "Confessor" for the way it straddled the line between religious and criminal confessions. For a visual, we wanted something that said both "priest" and "superhero," and eventually found it by combining a ninja mask with some outré priest's robes — but not before Alex tried dozens of masks, from influences as varied as opera, medieval armor and Dick Sprang.

Altar Boy came faster, once we combined a choirboy's robe with a Musketeer's surplice. And, of course, Alex worked out distinctive, involving faces for both of them.

EITHER WHITE PONCHO W/ CROSS ON FRONT UNDERGARMENT BLACK

GOLD TRIM

GOLD CROSS

CONFESSOR LOOKS LIKE GOLGOL 13 WITH WHITE HAIR

ear pieces on
goggles

metal yoke
design

strap
couterbelts

metal
presser

The Gunslinger was difficult in that we wanted a number of contrasting elements. He's half-Vietnamese, taking on the look of an American icon — but his look also needed to be a hi-tech twist on a period costume. Kurt asked for something that took the image of a dandified gunfighter and replaced all the turquoise and silver with circuitry, but Brent's first try (above) was too muted. So Kurt did one of the sketches that makes everyone glad he's a writer (above right), and Brent reworked it into something attractive and distinctive — one

Ironhorse was created, at least at first, to give Rex someone to arm-wrestle with, and in looking for a visual idea to contrast with Rex's saurian look, we hit on a mechanical hero. Kurt came up with the name "Ironhorse, the Human Locomotive," which in turn suggested a 19th century hero, and everything coalesced around that. Visually, he was somewhat tricky — steam engine elements were easy enough to find, but reworking them into a human form that looked both impressive and old-fashioned took some delicate design work.

GIVE HIM BROW-RIDGE

HEAD LARGER

SINK HEAD IN

SEE FIRE INSIDE

5 HEADS TALL

slots for expression

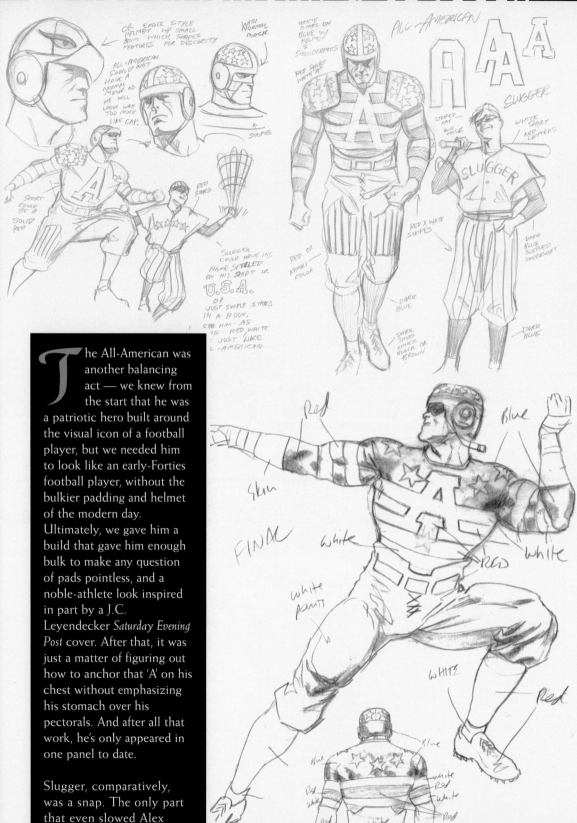

OR EAGLE STYLE HELMET W/ SMALL BRIM WHICH SHADES FEATURES FOR OBSCURITY

WITH NORMAL MASK

ALL-AMERICAN SHOULD NOT HAVE A NORMAL MASK AS HE WILL LOOK WAY TOO MUCH LIKE CAP.

STRIPES

SHIRT COULD BE A SOLID RED

RED STARS

SLUGGER COULD HAVE HIS NAME SPELLED ON HIS SHIRT OR

U.S.A.

OR JUST SIMPLE STARS IN A ROW, SEE HIM AS ... NG RED WHITE ... JUST LIKE ...-AMERICAN

WHITE STARS ON BLUE W/ HELMET & SHOULDERPADS

RED SHIRT WHITE "A"

ALL-AMERICAN

A A A

STRIPED HAT BLUE MASK

SLUGGER

WHITE SHIRT RED LETTERS

RED OR KHAKI COLOR

RED & WHITE STRIPES

DARK BLUE SLEEVED UNDERSHIRT

DARK BLUE

DARK SHOES EITHER BLACK OR BROWN

DARK BLUE

The All-American was another balancing act — we knew from the start that he was a patriotic hero built around the visual icon of a football player, but we needed him to look like an early-Forties football player, without the bulkier padding and helmet of the modern day. Ultimately, we gave him a build that gave him enough bulk to make any question of pads pointless, and a noble-athlete look inspired in part by a J.C. Leyendecker *Saturday Evening Post* cover. After that, it was just a matter of figuring out how to anchor that 'A' on his chest without emphasizing his stomach over his pectorals. And after all that work, he's only appeared in one panel to date.

Slugger, comparatively, was a snap. The only part that even slowed Alex down was the question of what to put on the front his uniform shirt...

Red

Blue

Skin

FINAL

White

White PANTS

RED

White

WHITE

Red

Blue

Blue

Red White

White Red White

Red

White

Red

COVER GALLERY

Glowing

MAUE FLEET
COMING IN
FROM TOP
INSTEAD OF
BOTTOM

ABOUT THE CREATORS

KURT BUSIEK broke into comics in 1982, selling stories to both DC and Marvel within weeks of finishing college. Since then, he's been an editor, a literary agent, a sales manager and more, but is best known as the multiple-award-winning writer of ASTRO CITY, MARVELS, SUPERMAN, ARROWSMITH, SUPERSTAR, SHOCKROCKETS, CONAN, and many others. He lives in the Pacific Northwest with his family.

BRENT ANDERSON began to write and draw his own comics in junior high school, and graduated to professional work less than a decade later. He's drawn such projects as KA-ZAR THE SAVAGE, X-MEN: GOD LOVES MAN KILLS, STRIKEFORCE: MORITURI, SOMERSET HOLMES, RISING STARS and, of course, ASTRO CITY, for which he's won multiple Eisner and Harvey Awards. He makes his home in Northern California.

ALEX ROSS worked on TERMINATOR: THE BURNING EARTH and Clive Barker's HELLRAISER before his breakout series, MARVELS, made him an overnight superstar. Since then, he's painted, plotted and/or written such series as KINGDOM COME, SUPERMAN: PEACE ON EARTH, JUSTICE, EARTH X, AVENGERS/INVADERS and PROJECT SUPERPOWERS, and won over two dozen industry awards.

WILL BLYBERG started out publishing and contributing to fanzines, before breaking in as an inker on books such as AMERICOMICS, DNAGENTS and AIRBOY. His inks have graced such series as ACTION COMICS, DEATHSTROKE, NEW TITANS and WONDER WOMAN, and he's teamed with Brent on ANIMA, GEN13, NIGHT FORCE and STAR WARS, in addition to ASTRO CITY.

ALEX SINCLAIR has colored virtually every DC character in existence, and more besides. Best known for his award-winning work with Jim Lee and Scott Williams, he's done color art for such books as BATMAN: HUSH, SUPERMAN: FOR TOMORROW, BLACKEST NIGHT, BATMAN & ROBIN, JLA, IDENTITY CRISIS, ARROWSMITH and more.

JOHN G. ROSHELL joined Comicraft in 1992, helping propel the lettering/design studio to its dominant position in the industry. As Senior Design Wizard, he's lettered thousands of comics pages, along with creating logos and fonts, designing book editions and more. He also writes the series CHARLEY LOVES ROBOTS, which appears in ELEPHANTMEN.

RICHARD STARKINGS dimly remembers working on some BATMAN project... THE KILLING JOKE? People insist that he did letter it with a tool not unlike a computer... but too many lattes and British chocolate has wiped his recollections of anything prior to Illustrator 5. He currently writes ELEPHANTMEN.